Communication in
the Analects of Confucius

PETER LANG
PROMPT

PETER LANG
New York • Bern • Berlin
Brussels • Vienna • Oxford • Warsaw

Francisco García Marcos

Communication in
the Analects of Confucius

PETER LANG

New York • Bern • Berlin

Brussels • Vienna • Oxford • Warsaw

Library of Congress Cataloging-in-Publication Control Number 2022028010

Bibliographic information published by **Die Deutsche Nationalbibliothek**.
Die Deutsche Nationalbibliothek lists this publication in the "Deutsche
Nationalbibliografie"; detailed bibliographic data are available
on the Internet at http://dnb.d-nb.de/.

ISBN 978-1-4331-9257-9 (hardcover)
ISBN 978-1-4331-9496-2 (ebook pdf)
ISBN 978-1-4331-9497-9 (epub)
DOI 10.3726/b19360

This publication has been peer reviewed and meets
the highest quality standards for content and production.

© 2022 Francisco García Marcos

Peter Lang Publishing, Inc., New York
80 Broad Street, 5th floor, New York, NY 10004
www.peterlang.com

To Jian Zou, for his dear friendship

Contents

List of Figures and Tables

Figures

Tables

Introduction

The thought of approaching the work of Confucius (孔夫子; Kǒngfuzǐ) is both a thrill and a challenge. It is a thrill because the reader is approaching one of the great references of thinking in human history. For this very reason, it is also a challenge for the writer, as he or she must try to make the most of such a profound wealth of reflection and human knowledge. Therefore, considering writing about any aspect of this work implies an enormous responsibility by all means. For centuries, Confucius received continuous attention from scholars all over the world. At times, one feels the legitimate vertigo of not finding anything substantial to contribute to such a vast and intense legacy.

To do so in a little-trodden subject, as is the case with communication, is perhaps daring. In any case, my approach comes from a deep admiration for a system of thinking which, with all the precautions and nuances that distance in time demands, is one of the pinnacles of human knowledge. I also write from the honesty of being sincerely convinced that communication is one of the facets worth exploring within the Confucian universe. That is my purpose in the pages that follow.

The presence of a certain communicative component in the Analects and in the overall Confucian perspective has had its fluctuations in the specialised bibliography, always within the very modest quotas of attention. Although it has been relatively common to refer to some passages linked to the use of languages, this has not prevented the emergence of objections of varying magnitude. For Guoxi (2009) this is neither an easy nor an immediate task. He warns about the polysemy of the term "speak" in the ancient classical tradition of Chinese thinking, not always directly equivalent to its current uses, even less so within the Western tradition. So much so that he distinguishes at least five semantic levels in traditional Chinese "speaking", which would correspond to the contents of "fact", "knowledge", "truth", "sense" or "thing". For Gouxi, the verbal activity (speaking) in Confucius unfolds on the first three levels. This is only partially true. As it will be further discussed, Lu's teacher incorporates other dimensions of communicative activity, directly related to the social activity of the exemplary individual.

Chang (1997) seems even less convinced that Confucius' work has an intrinsic interest in language and communication. The presence of such issues in the literature would not be due to the core of the Confucian contribution, but to what he considers to be an insistence on extracting social readings from Confucius. Therefore, he advocates a relatively limited list of concerns, concentrating on the word as a referent of morality, the censorship of verbal ornamentation, the rules governing verbal decorum and the preponderance of acts over their linguistic manifestations. It is true that Chang (1997) seems more interested in criticising the communication of what he calls "Confucian societies" than really getting into the communicative question within the Confucian conceptual universe.

However, this has not always been the case, especially since 2000. The bibliography also includes more specific approaches to language and communication in Confucian texts. These studies have at least provided a general framework on which to build more specific future research. Kejian (2002) and Jiaqian (2005) make a general approach to the linguistic issue in Confucius. Zhiping and Yanyun (2004), on the other hand, address the issue of the ownership of language use from the Confucian perspective. Yongkai (2001) and Lei (2007) deal with the rectification of names, one of the central themes in Chinese philosophy at the time. Quiao and Min (2009) take a more specific approach to the projection of language within Confucius' philosophical scheme. They distinguish three main functions. At the base, it would act as a transmitter of communication, on which the other two, its ethical and political functions, are based.

Of course, I respectfully but firmly disagree with these perspectives. I have approached the Analects on several occasions, although I have only now finished giving it a systematic format. During this time, my conviction that language occupies a nuclear place in the ethical system developed in the work has been reaffirmed. By using the word "nuclear", I do not mean the key to explaining the whole of Confucius' intellectual legacy. I do mean that, in any case, it is associated with the major issues addressed therein, playing a determining role, both in its delimitation and in its projection towards social dynamics.

Certainly, the 2020 paper was not my first attempt to approach this side of the Confucian legacy either. I have always been inclined to place myself on the side of the linguistic light within the *Analects*. In García Marcos (2008) included an entire chapter devoted to linguistic reflections in Ancient China. The imperative of sticking to strict historiographical reality served to bring me back to one of my usual readings, the *Analects* of Confucius. In 2019 I managed to go a step further and close this first monographic reflection on the topic of communication in the work and thinking of Confucius. The purpose got off to a rather unflattering start. The publishers considered the work to be a novel, a judgement that touched considerably my personal esteem for reasons that are easy to understand. Fortunately, the text reached Javier Campos Daroca who, far from considering it as such, encouraged me to continue with this line of research. Of course, the word of a wise man was enough to heal the wounds.

Therefore, it may be understood that I am tented to forgo any kind of standard introduction. I am firmly persuaded that they run the serious risk of becoming tedious fragments mainly used to justify the obvious: that an author has decided to write about the subject that the reader has in his hands. There is no more worthy or more beautiful justification for both the act of writing and reading. Writers and readers are brought together in the pages of a book fundamentally because they have decided to do so. They may have been moved by an irrational impulse, a hidden complicity, shared intellectual interests, the will to progress in the knowledge of a subject, an unexpected chance, perhaps an eye-catching cover – anything. In the end, it doesn't matter what or why.

So, without any remorse, I prefer not to look for the paths of my trajectory that have led me to China, Confucius, the *Analects* and communication. I don't consider any details of my bland biography to be of any interest at all. I am convinced that if someone has reached these pages, it is not exactly because of me, but because of what I have written and is announced in the title.

I am neither willing to exaggerate the disciplinary justification of this work, especially in our time, when linguistics has more than ostensibly broadened its interests. Therefore, there is every reason for a professor of general linguistics to take up these matters. Perhaps those who are familiar with my professional background may be surprised that I am not fiddling with sociolects or snippets of the history of linguistics. In any case, I am not entirely sure that I have completely neglected my main disciplinary concerns. Addressing the linguistic and communicative question in Confucius, in fact, does not cease to delve into a substantial part of the linguistic history of antiquity. However, without losing this general reference, I intend to focus on the perspective that the Analects convey about language and communication.

Otherwise, I must admit that the analects of Confucius have been constant companions on my personal journey through my life. Like a magnet, both fortunate and gratifying, I have always drawn lessons from them. They made me rethink many of the concepts I took for granted. So rethinking communication in the light of Confucius and vice versa has already happened to me once, in 2019, as it has happened again at the present time. The results are the reflections that are recorded here which will try to confirm or refute the hypotheses of my previous incursion into this problematic, without disdaining the possibility of new ones appearing.

Neither before nor now have I tried to become a sinologist because I do not consider it to be so extraordinarily conveying. I am a humble and simple citizen, a linguist by profession who tells what he has seen, thought or understood in relation to that subject. Moreover, I am convinced that this is a way of doing justice to Confucius, the millenary master of Lu. His reflection is of such a human depth that it also admits Western readings from eyes unversed in Sinological traditions, thousands of years away, but which continue to find knowledge and humanity in his words. That is why Confucius is not only a master of Lu, but in my modest opinion, he is a master from Lu.

On this long road of my interest in Confucius and his work, I must express my gratitude to many people, starting with my brother Alberto, my first teacher in oriental thinking, and continuing with my colleague and friend Pedro San Ginés, a true reference in Spanish sinology. The infinite understanding of my family, who suffered in these circumstances, has allowed me to write this work. In any case, it would never have reached port without so many dear friends in Almería, Granada, Barcelona and Poland, who are able to forgive me for anything, even for daring to write about Confucius.

Almería, spring 2021
Francisco García Marcos

References

Chang, H. C. (1997). Language and words: Communication in the Analects of Confucius. *Journal of Language and Social Psychology, 16*(2), 107-131.

Feng J. (2005). A brief study on Confucius' views on Language. *Journal of Guangxi Radio and TV University, 11*, 37-40.

García Marcos, F. (2009). *Aspectos de historia social de la lingüística. (I) De la Antigüedad al siglo XIX*. Barcelona: Octaedro.

———. (2019). *Cuando comunicar es actuar*. Almería: Círculo Rojo.

Guoxi, D. (2009). The discussion of Confucius on Speech. *Guan Zi Journal*, (3), 15.

Jiaqian, F. (2005). A brief study on Confucius' views on Language. *Journal of Guangxi Radio and TV University, 11*, 37-40.

Kejian, L. (2002). A study on Confucius' views on Language. *Journal of Hexi Normal University, 6*, 57-60.

Lei, W. (2007). A study on Confucius' rectification of names. *Information of Culture and Education, 2*, 92–93.

Qiao, L., & Min, S. (2009). A study on Confucius' views on Language Functions. ポリグロシア, *16*, 69-75.

Yongkai, L. (2001). A comparison on Confucius' and Laozi's views on language. *Study on Confucius, 4*, 56-61.

Zhiping, Z., & Yanyun, H. (2004). Confucius' concept of speech appropriacy. *Journal of Jiangxi Institute of Education (Social Sciences), 25*, 70-72.

1

The Analects: Their Time, Their Environment and Their Projection

The history and the social relevance of the Confucian *Analects* is well known and referred to both in the strictly specialised bibliography and even among other more popular works. They are known as the *Four Books*, texts that make up the historical canon of Confucian philosophy. Alongside them figure the *Book of Mencius*, probably Confucius's most beloved disciple, *The Great Teaching* and the *Righteous Middle Way*. All of them must have been compiled between the 7th and 3rd century B.C. and were available when the First Emperor Qin (221 B.C.) begins the great unification of China, overcoming a relatively obscure period in the country's more immediate history. From then on, they became a formative reference for the whole country.

It is very likely that the initial configuration of the work itself was partially the result of a collective work. In any case, it is certain that over the centuries its enormous influence on Chinese society and its secular transmission has granted a propitious occasion for the insertion of multiple commentaries that have necessarily tinged the original texts with the perspectives that each era has added to them. This influence should not always be seen in strictly negative terms. On the contrary, it should be interpreted as a manifestation of the vitality of an approach that was able to remain valid over time, which inevitably entailed its corresponding and periodic updates, no more or less than for several millennia.

1.1 The *Rújiā*

In any case, the *Four Books* as a whole, to which the *Analects* will be added, formed the core of what will be known as the *School of the Learned*, in its translation into Western languages, the Chinese *Rújiā*. Confucius, his doctrine and his legacy. It includes his disciples integrated into this school, which constituted an educated stratum of traditional Chinese society, learned in the liberal arts and knowledge of the classics and specialised in rituals.

Nevertheless, this attribution, which is almost immediate and inevitable in the literature, is met with a certain amount of caution. De Prada (2015: 52–54) recommends caution due to the inherent limitations that the translation of Chinese into alphabetic languages usually entails. He notes this in relation to the term that defines this school, 儒家, "rújiā", which he proposes to examine in detail in the original Chinese (De Prada, 2015: 52–54). About 家, "jiā", he does not harbour too many doubts, since it refers to "those who are gathered around a teacher" and, therefore, to "school". Doubts arise when translating 儒, "rú", as "learned". A first literal approach would provide a translation as "man who invokes rain for the plants that have just sprouted from the earth", from which we propose to accept that we are dealing with "necessary men", given that rain is an essential element for the growth of vegetation. Therefore, it is about the school of men that a society needs for its correct development and functioning, meaning those who generate harmony among their contemporaries.

Levi (2002: 111), meanwhile, had made several interpretations of the term "rú", only partly coinciding with the previous ones, by making it equivalent to "weak", "docile", "preceptor", "instructor", "literate", "enlightened", "impregnated" (of men and good ideas), "duty" and "contortionist" (figuratively, as a person who handles arguments). "rú", "literate", "enlightened", "imbued" (with men and good ideas), "duty" and "contortionist" (figuratively, as a person who handles arguments). Eno (1990: 190–198) emphasised a meaning analogous to the latter, when he proposes to translate it as "clown", as a person who earns the appreciation of others through his skills. In all these versions, several main ideas converge about the "rú" as a person with a specific social identity, whose activity lays on interaction with other individuals, from whom he earns their favour and respect.

Indeed, the members of this school seem to have constituted a formal and recognisable stratum within Chinese society, even though today it is relatively difficult to delimit its notional scope. In theory, they should have specialised in knowledge of ritual, the liberal arts and classical authors. The disciples of Confucius are part of this social group, although not exclusively so (Levi, 2018: 100–106). It is true that Confucius formalised many of the defining traits of the literati, meanwhile making them a guide for the formation of elites. However, they were more people involved in that endeavour.

In any case, as Levi (2018: 112–113) reminds, the probable existence of other literati should not make us lose the reference to the scholastic character of the Confucian legacy; not only the existence of a doctrinal corpus and of some followers, directly according to many testimonies, but also in terms of the maintenance of the doctrine that many other disciples will follow through time.

1.2 Background to Chinese Thought and History

This group of experts, who in the Western society would basically be classified as philosophers and ethicists, played a crucial role in the China of that time, with extraordinary repercussions later. But the foundations of Chinese thought had been laid several millennia earlier. There was an ancient mythology, a complete cosmogony, scrupulously determined rites and habits, and a historical trajectory delimited with its corresponding periods.

For traditional Chinese cosmogony (Birrell, 1999; Kalinowksi, 1991), in the beginning there was only black and formless chaos, black. It took eighteen thousand years to merge, creating a cosmic egg. Inside it, yin and yang coexisted together with Pangu, who would become the demiurge in charge of elaborating the known world and life. Emerging from this cosmic entity, he proceeded to separate these two principles with his giant axe. From yang he formed Heaven. From yin he made Earth. In any case, it was necessary to separate the two elements, for which another eighteen thousand years were needed, pushing the yang upwards and the yin downwards every day. Having achieved this, he lay down to rest and to die weary and old. His expiration became the source of life. The mountains came from his body, the rivers from his blood, the farmlands from his muscles, the stars and the firmament from his beard, the forests from his hair and, finally, the minerals, especially the valuable ones, from his bones. His death created more things. His breath gave birth to the wind, his voice was the origin of thunder, from his left eye the sun sprouted and from his right the moon appeared. His sweat was transformed into rain, and the little beings that were sheltered in his body were finally transformed into humans by the action of the wind.

As in so many other human civilizations, the corresponding religious practices, as well as a mythological lineage, were immediately derived from that nuclear cosmology. That made it possible to explain and justify the origin of the known history. Apparently, the first rites had a magical origin, promoting communication between the Human Being and those telluric forces of the Universe. The conviction was harboured that most phenomena were governed from a distance by spirits. This genesis was partially maintained since they were systematically used to defend themselves from evil,[1] communicate with spirits,[2] divine the future[3] or even to try to modify it.[4] Thus, both the rites and the sacrifices ended up creating something similar to a religion that, in any case, did not prevent the development of other civic and moral values. Thus, from remote antiquity China had had a doctrinal corpus of theological beliefs and a considerably established ethical standard.

As it progressed, mythology sustained the start of the Chinese historical genealogy itself. The first dynasties, which could be dated around the III millennium B.C., were the successors of Pangu. The August Three—also known as the Sublime Emperors[5]—and the Five Legendary

1 Through mirrors, the true image of evil spirits is captured allowing protection from them. At the same time, the possession of one of these mirrors guaranteed heavenly happiness.
2 Among other procedures, the one known as automatic writing stands out. Questions were written on a paper to the spirits who are on the other side (supposedly from death). After burning these questions, the medium proceeded to answer them unconsciously, writing with a peach branch on a box full of sand.
3 Numerous procedures were used for this. Inscriptions containing divinatory rituals were made on tortoise shells or ox bones. It must have been a very widespread procedure, judging by the abundant archaeological documentation recorded. Since Wang Yirong and Liu E discovered the first remains in 1899, more than 200,000 samples have appeared. On other occasions, fire, facial features, palmistry, divinatory sticks and the Chinese horoscope were used. Their popularity continues to this day, already throughout the world.
4 Spells of various kinds were performed aiming at influencing the actions that could condition the life of humans. One of the most referred to is to write in dark red ink on normal yellow or red paper. For this, a special calligraphy is used, using a pencil made with peach wood. Once the text is written, it is placed on a door or hidden in the hair. In its strictest version, it can be burned, to mix its ashes in tea or water. Ingested, they transmit protection to the entire body of the individual.
5 As in all mythological literature, it is likely that they were inspired by tribal chiefs, famous warriors or relevant figures of their time, to which the collective imagination

Sovereigns[6] carried out this foundational task. Under his mandate the first institutions would have developed, which would have allowed the progressive settlement of society. The origins of traditional medicine and the calendar also come from that mythical time, as well as the ethical and moral principles that guide social life. It is important to highlight the role played by the sovereign in this regard, already from this early stage in Chinese history. The political vertex of the country embodies in its own person the virtues that it demands from its people and that are ultimately the parameters by which it is governed. This reflection of the high social orders in daily life will reach later stages of Chinese thought and will have a more than relevant role. Naturally, the distance between what morality advised and the practice of everyday life was more than considerable in more than a few moments, becoming a source of conflicts and historical contradictions.

Of course, any historical identification of these monarchs is ruled out, although this is still a secondary circumstance. The determining factor is that social and cultural bases that will find a remarkable consistency and shape the present and future reality of the country are established.

The Five Emperors were followed by the Xia dynasty (2207 B.C.–1766 B.C.), with documented history.[7] Founded by Yu, *the Great*, it introduced some elements that would have an extraordinary impact on Chinese history. Yu seems to

added everything else. Of centuries-old lives, in addition to enormous military victories, even miraculous events are attributed to them. There are several versions about who exactly made up that triad. Fu Xi and Shennong are in all of them. On the third member there is already more diversification: Suiren, Nüwa or Gòngong. The reference of classical Chinese historiography, Sima Qian (145 B.C.–90 B.C.), opts for more generic names: The Celestial Augustus, the Earthly Augustus and the Augustus Tài.

6 About the Five Emperors there seems to be a greater relative agreement, with a roster made up of Huangdi —the Yellow Emperor—Zhan Xu, Di Ku, Yao and Shun. However, it is not the only option either. In the Elegies of Chu, a poetic anthology from the 3rd century B.C., they are identified with the five cardinal points, including the center as the fifth of those elements.

7 At least in a very substantial part. For a long time, the strict historicity of this dynasty was doubted. But in 1928 the first sites were found at Anyang, followed by those at Erlitou in 1959, both in what is now the Chinese province of Henan. Carbon-14 dates this civilization to between 2100 B.C. and 1800 B.C. It would correspond to the reigns that lasted from the 21st century B.C. to the 16th century B.C. Sima Qian, one of the great historians of ancient China, mentions seventeen monarchs before the emergence of the Shang dynasty.

have been a solid military man, victorious in the many conflicts that shook the borders of China at the time. But he is also portrayed as an outstanding manager, credited with the design of canals that prevented the periodic flooding of the great Yellow River. He also established a monarchy of hereditary succession, the origin of his own dynasty. But, as far as we are concerned, he is considered a firm believer in the cultivation of human virtues. In particular, he advocated that man should be open-hearted (but avoid excessive and unwarranted generosity), flexible (but firm at the same time), simple (but still dignified), inclined to order (but still respectful), accommodating (but avoid weakness), upright (combined with gentleness), avoid pettiness (but with care), act severely (but only in cases where reason indicates) and proceed to act in a strong and just manner. The sum of these virtues was to lead to perfection of being, to the ideal model of personal identity and behaviour.

There are three features that should not be overlooked in this ethos of Yu, founder of the Xia dynasty (Yan-Hun, 2008). On the one hand, it is a list of weighted, balanced and even nuanced virtues. Yu seems to shy away from drastic extremes, preferring a balance that holds things together. From the sum of these virtues follows an overcoming of human limitations at the outset and it constitutes the form of a path to perfection. Finally, the sovereign himself becomes a reference point for his subjects, from whom he expects an imitation of this virtuous ideal. In any case it should not be overlooked that this ethical programme is still a kind of desideratum, which did not find such immediate practice in a society which was a slave society after all. The ex-post effectiveness of the desideratum was that it eventually became an ideal model that was passed on to future generations.

Around 1600 B.C. China underwent another great transformation, this time with the rise of the Shang dynasty[8] (Allan, 1984). Hailing from the lands bordering the Yellow River, the basis of their economy was based on agriculture, hunting, animal husbandry and military disputes with their neighbours ensued. It seems that they were highly ritualistic, especially in honouring the memory of their ancestors and their spirits (Smith, 1961). Archaeological sites have yielded oracular eggs in considerable quantity. They must have believed in something similar to another existence after death. Valuable objects have been found in their graves, presumably for use in that other reality after the passage through life.

---

8 That on this occasion it has been historically documented without major drawbacks, thanks to its secure appearance in the Shujing (*Book of History*), as well as in the Liji (*Book of Rites*) and the Shijing (*Book of Odes*).

Remains of human beings have also been found buried alive, a sign of the survival of the slavery inherited from the previous period. The Shang were defeated at the Battle of Mu, around 1046 B.C. (Eberhard, 2013; Fairbank, 1978).

This date marks the beginning of the Zhou dynasty. But it also meant something else. This shift from a corrupt dynasty—the Shang—to a seemingly virtuous one—the Zhou—was considered as a mandate from Heaven. That has two important consequences on the immediate mentality: to persevere and reaffirm the conviction that it is essential to guarantee the imperious exemplarity of the sovereign and to nourish the idea that Heaven disposes and decides the fate of men and societies. As on so many other occasions, inside and outside China, in remote stages or in more recent events, reality will impose more than considerable nuances.

The Zhou, coming from the upper reaches of the Yellow River, ruled China from then until 221 B.C., thus becoming the longest historical dynasty of that period at that time; a feudal society was established with important foundations of Chinese thought and art. Probably because of this longevity, it experienced two clearly differentiated periods. Up to 771 B.C. is the time of the so-called Western Zhou. Historians speak of a strong government, mainly centralised around the nuclear city of Fēng (Roberts, 2011). From then on, the Eastern Zhou began, until 256 B.C., with a merely symbolic power and a huge dispersion within a clearly convulsive history. In Chinese historiography, this last stage consists of the periods of the Springs and Autumns (722 B.C.–481 B.C.) and the Warring Kingdoms. The first period saw a strong decentralisation of power, with numerous conflicts, which resulted in a varied transit of kingdoms moving in, out and around the Chinese map, and consequent atomisation at all levels. Despite this, an unknown expansion of culture, including a significant increase in literacy among the lower strata of the population, was registered. From the end of this period until 221 B.C., all these trends intensified and the decline of central power increased even further, until the definitive arrival of the Qin dynasty.

References

Birrell, A. (1999). *Chinese mythology: An introduction.* Baltimore/London: Johns Hopkins University Press.

De Prada García, A. (2015). Confucio y la escuela de los letrados: humanidad y armonía. *La Albolafia: Revista de Humanidades y Cultura,* (4), 51-64.

Eberhard, W. (2013). *A history of China.* London: Routledge.

Eno, R. 1990. *The Confucian Creation of Heaven.* New York: State University of New York Press.

Fairbank, J. K. (1978). *The Cambridge History of China* (Vol. 1). Cambridge: Cambridge University Press.

Kalinowski, M. (1991). *Cosmology et divination dans la Chine ancienne: Le Compendium des Cinq Agents (Wuxing dayi, Vie siècle).* Paris: École Française d'Extrê me-Orient.

Levi, J. (2002). *Confucius.* Paris: Pygmalion.

———. (2018). Les assassins de Confucius. Du négationnisme dans la sinologie américaine contemporaine. 2018. halshs-01881797 (Access: 26-12-2017).

2

Confucius, Historical Figure and Cultural Myth

2.1 Confucius and His Time

Kǒngzǐ, transcribed as Confucius, was born in 551 B.C., in Zou, in the state of Lu, in north-eastern China (the present-day province of Shangdong). Therefore, he lived in the middle of the Spring and Autumn period.

There is no need to insist in the central role that the figure of Confucius has played in Chinese tradition and thought. To begin with, he has inspired a remarkable heterogeneity of deep questions. The Analects deal with foundational approaches to society, its governance, the cohesive dynamics of human groups, the performance of individuals within them and, closely related to this last aspect, the training necessary to become an exemplary person. Thus, the figure of Confucius brings together the dimension of the politician, the educator, the philosopher and, as a summary of all this, also that of the upright and virtuous citizen.

Probably because of this intense heterogeneity, it is immediately worth remembering that Confucius also became the starting point of a crucial line of Chinese thought, inside the aforementioned *Rújiā*. As noted above, it has been discussed that its extent and the extent to which Confucius and his disciples were part of it, whether it can be restricted to Confucianism or whether it was part of a wider movement. In any case, what is certain is that these authors, his disciples, preserved the doctrinal foundations of Confucianism and transmitted it in such an efficient way that it has undoubtedly constituted one of the great traditional pillars of Chinese culture and, by extension, of universal thought.

Given the extraordinary dimension of his figure, and the distance in time between 6th century B.C. and the present day, it is difficult to have a completely uniform picture of the strictly historical figure of Confucius. In fact, three major biographical sources are accepted, each of them highlighting specific aspects of his personality. The Analects were collected by the master's direct disciples and early followers in the centuries immediately after his death. Among them, the figure of the one who is concerned with the correct moral behaviour of the individual, in practically all facets of life, is fundamentally emphasised. Moral rectitude admits of no restrictions, nor it is conditioned in any way.

The following two biographical sources date from around the 4th century B.C. Confucius is conveniently included in the Zuozhuan, the earliest Chinese narrative history, whose authorship is not fully established. Traditionally attributed to Zuo Qiuming, a court writer contemporary with Confucius in Lu, scholars today seem more inclined to regard it as a work composed in several phases and by several authors. In addition to being a prose reference, it is certain that it reports the period between 722 B.C. and 468 B.C. The Zuozhuan mystified the figure of Confucius, who became a guarantor of Lu, his birthplace, considerably endangered.

The Confucius of Mencius, the last reference of this triad, concentrates on the profile of the politician, the prominent position in the administration and the paths leading to it. This writer is one of the most enthusiastic followers of the master's teachings.

To these three accounts can be added an unspecified number of legends about him, as well as Chapter X of the *Analects* itself, traditionally considered autobiographical. All of them eventually converge in the biography included in the Records of the Great Historian, probably composed between 109 B.C. and 91 B.C. They are concluded by Sima Qian (145 B.C.–90 B.C.), an official at the court of the Han dynasty. However, it seems that it was his father, the astrologer Sima Tan (165 B.C.–110 B.C.), who started the writing of the work. It covers 2500 years of Chinese history, from the legendary age of Huangdi (2717 B.C.–2599 B.C.), the Yellow Emperor, to the age contemporary to the author, not without abundant references to the rest of the known world. In it, largely following the Zuozhuan, a family genealogy of Confucius is given which is not unanimously accepted. According to Sima Qian, Confucius' family came to Lu when his great-grandfather left his hometown of Song, which was in turmoil at the time.

There, in south-eastern Shandong, around the present-day city of Qufu, the family, former noble landowners related to the Song duchy (Levi, 2012: 101), ends up impoverished. However, still according to Sima Qian's account, his father Shu failed to regain the family status, despite having been at the head of the Lu army in 563 B.C. and 556 B.C. His premature death, when Confucius was barely three years old, plunged the family back into a delicate economic situation. On the other hand, little is known of Confucius' mother, except that she may have belonged to the Yan family.

Little is known about his early years. Sima Qian describes him as a young man from a humble background, who in his early years guarded livestock and kept accounts in Lu's granaries. This did not prevent him from receiving a conscientious and careful education, despite his early paternal orphanage (Chin, 2007; Prevosti, Del Río & Prats, 2014). That made him trained in the knowledge of ritual, music and thought.

He entered the Lu state administration at a very young age. There, he reached the rank of what today would be, roughly speaking, a Minister of Justice. He resigned because of his profound disagreements with the prince. This episode is an example of the profound disenchantment of a large part of the Chinese intellectuality at the time.

Being part of the Lu administration did not come without risks. Firstly, because of the configuration of the state: three families of the same clan, the Huan, were inherited to their main positions, which led to constant instability. Secondly, during the Zou dynasty there was a progressive and unstoppable degradation of social life, which reached really high levels. In addition to a radical distrust of the rulers, there was an intense distrust of the gods, who seemed to have abandoned China as well. Cultural historians stress that this was a period far removed from religion and divine beliefs (Barreno, 2017; Roberts, 2011). Perhaps not in a radical way, but it did at least attenuate the consistency of religious beliefs, in the face of such helplessness.

What is certain is that political disorder sheltered wars and violence in a tumultuous climate in which citizens moved between fear and bewilderment. Therefore, it is not surprising that the most pressing task of philosophers was to find a guiding principle for life and society, a parameter by which to orient behaviour and the very personality of everyone.

Again, Confucius is a paradigmatic example in this respect. In 517 B.C. Duke Zhao revolted against this order by confronting the Ji, the most powerful faction. The failure of this attempt forced the duke into exile, first in the neighbouring state of Qi and later in Jin. Confucius apparently accompanied Zhao and entered the service of the Qi nobility. However, he returned to Lu, where he made some notable interventions. The sources do not fully clarify the level of Confucius' positions in Lu, although they are almost unanimously inclined to consider them relatively modest. According to the Zuozhuan, his most prominent administrative service must have taken place in 500 B.C., during the meeting of Qi and Lu rulers at Jiayu to seal a peace agreement. Confucius assisted Duke Ding with remarkable skill. Not only did he succeed in preventing his state from being humiliated but he also regained part of the Lu territory that had passed into the hands of his rivals.

Lu's internal instability worked against him again. His new protector, the Duke of Ding, was embroiled in the internal struggles of the Huan families, with little success in his pretensions. Although Confucius was only partly involved in this court, some of his disciples were not, although they all ended up in exile. From 496 B.C. onwards he abandoned all his posts in Lu and began a fruitless search for an ideal ruler somewhere on the vast Chinese map—Wei, Song, Chen, Cai and Chu. Nor did he ever find a worthy occupation in which he could apply his knowledge. These were difficult years, with many disappointments, in which he suffered serious economic hardship, amidst unworthy and unexemplary rulers. Finally, in 484 B.C. he gave up his purpose and returned to Lu. Although he established some contact with the Ji, hegemonic in the complex family network of the state, from then on, he concentrated on teaching and revising classical texts, such as the *Book of Odes*, the *Book of Documents* and the *Spring and Autumn Annals*, which contain the court chronicle of Lu, as well as works on ritual and music. From that moment, this was his life's work, concentrating on writing and commenting on classical authors, as well as teaching, until his death in 479 B.C.

Through the biographical chronology of Confucius we gain access to numerous snippets about his personality. From very early on he is portrayed as a character endowed with great curiosity. The Zuozhuan mentions a visit to the state of Tan in 525, when he was only twenty-seven years old. There he already regretted all the traditional knowledge that had been lost and took a keen interest in history and the workings of the bureaucracy. This, of course, will be a constant in the *Analects*, which show the master always attentive and eager for knowledge.

Through the biographical chronology of Confucius, we gain access to numerous snippets about his personality. From very early on he is portrayed as a character endowed with great curiosity. The Zuozhuan mentions a visit to the state of Tan in 525, when he was only twenty-seven years old. There he already regretted the traditional knowledge that had been lost and took a keen interest in history and the works of the bureaucracy. This will, of course, be a constant in the Analects, which present the master as always attentive and eager for knowledge.

The biographical notes from the sources already highlight his ability to adapt to the circumstances. He is portrayed as a person of modest habits in his intimate environment who, nevertheless, does not shirk the appropriate rigour required for formal occasions. His hobbies include music, which he records in the Analects. The fundamentals of these traits of Confucius' personality have come to form almost a biographical canon that has survived almost to the present day, also present in more contemporary portraits of his figure (Chin, 2009; Sarkissian, H. 2010; Tan, 2014).

In any case, it seems to be documented that he enjoyed only relative social success among his contemporaries. It is true that Sima Qian attributed to him more than three thousand followers in his time, a rather unlikely figure. Mencius reduced them to no more than seventy-two. This assessment is more in line with the impression conveyed from the Zuozhuan, where it was suggested that Confucius had not received in his lifetime the high recognition he deserved. Mencius, in the 4th century B.C., saw in his master an exceptional being. But such a reading would take time to become widespread. Above all, during the dominance of the Qin dynasty, his teachings were outlawed in the 3rd century B.C. The Han dynasty restored the intellectual legacy of Confucius, to the point that by the middle of the 2nd century B.C. they had become official. In the 3rd, Xunzi (313-238 B.C.) reserved a prominent place for him among the masters. One hundred years later he was already an undisputed figure, as one of the great references of universal thought, Chinese particularly.

2.2 The Doctrines of Confucius

2.2.1 Conceptual Framework

De Prada (2015: 54–56), after an etymological analysis of the characters that preside over Confucian temples even today -天 地 君 親 師-, establishes a semantic universe concentrated around five factors. Two of them were linked to nature (the sky and the earth), another two referred to the social fabric (the family and the teachers), united by a fifth element, the central figure of his conceptual cosmos, the king. In this way, the figure of the monarch acts as a weighting and balancing element for the forces of nature and mankind.

Of course, in this conceptual universe, some of the main lines that will be repeated in more specific and concrete aspects of his position are set out: the figure of the monarch acquires a transcendental dimension, beyond the fact that he holds political power, as a reference point for everything that concerns the life of his societies; the need to find a balanced weighting between the elements; the importance of the family as a cardinal element of social activity; education as an agent for the development of the individual and his correct insertion in the community.

However, the *Analects* are not primarily a doctrinal exposition of content. Confucius' aim is not to find a foundation for human existence in its correlation with the world, but rather to establish a guide of behavioural guidelines for the correct location and development of the individual within that universe.

2.2.2 The Alleged Religiosity of the Analects

All these elements end up providing a reading of the world, men and human relations. Therefore, at the outset there are no strong arguments to suggest that Confucius' reflections establish any form of recognisable religion, at least in common terms.

However, Confucianism has frequently figured in the lists of confessions professed by humankind since ancient times (Shih, 1970; Smith, 1963; Sommer, 1995; Wilson, 2020). So, at the same time, it has been inevitable to question the actual extent of religiosity in the Analects, and there have been conflicting views on this.

The controversy is based on the length of certain expressions in the Confucian work. Certainly, there is no lack of references to the "Mandate of Heaven", "Lord on High" or "Heaven". From there, a wide range of interpretations have been opened, attributing to Confucius' doctrinal corpus a monotheistic conception to a naturalistic pantheism, from an implicit polytheism to a quite considerable agnosticism.

Before making any pronouncements, it is necessary to gauge the real statistical weight of these references in the Analects as a whole. This makes it necessary to be more cautious about classifying Confucius as a religious man, a kind of prophet or great oriental theologian. Moreover, there are several reasons that point in this direction.

To begin with, religious references are not extraordinarily common in these pages. They are present, but neither are they the concepts on which Confucius insists most in the work. They lack any possible comparison with the continued relevance that he, master of Lu, employs when he speaks of "filial piety", "benevolence", the "Righteous Middle", "loyalty" or the "Superior Man", as the modern translation into Western languages prefers, a question to which I shall return in more detail.

To continue, the reference to religion is part of the received conceptual heritage. Text linguistics insists, when dealing with the mechanisms of coherence, on the importance of encyclopaedic knowledge, both when elaborating and decoding texts (De Beaugrande, 2011; De Beaugrande & Dressler, 1981; Foltz, Kintsch, & Landauer, 199; Halliday & Webster, 2014; Tierney & Mosenthal, 1983). It refers to the concepts, experiences and knowledge that form part of the baggage incorporated by any individual due to his or her ascription to a culture. The truth is that this encyclopaedic domain inherited by Confucius and his contemporaries had some deep-rooted clichés from ancient times. As indicated above, traditional Chinese was dominated by rites and their central role in social life, by the desirability of weight in actions, by the non-negotiable exemplarity of public figures and by the conviction that Heaven can determine the existence of men. When Confucius appeals to this, he is drawing on the cultural encyclopaedia shared with his interlocutors, which is also necessary to codify his messages as efficiently as possible. Of course, the effectiveness of his messages must have been a priority objective for a man like Confucius, committed to the improvement of his society through its members. Communicating properly was therefore not an option, but an imperative, although this will be returned to in much greater detail later.

The issue of alleged Confucian religiosity is of direct interest to me here, but for the exact opposite reasons. If we stick to the strict literality of the texts, it is not pertinent to raise any religious question. The *Analects* are not a theological treatise, a guide for believers or an exposition of transcendent truths, or even a reflection on the Divinity. All this is taken for granted, as something implicit and evident, which is part of the culture from which the author writes, and which is well known to the reader. In any case, there are truths of faith that are not addressed and developed, except in exceptional cases, only when they have some tangible transcription in social life.

Thus, it is no exaggeration to say that the Analects do not focus on theological questions, even though there are still some embers that support the opposite interpretation, that of a religious foundation. Certainly, Confucian ethics has sometimes been interpreted from these parameters, linked to a strong theological affiliation. According to this approach, insofar as the Human Being must act in accordance with what is ordained by Heaven, Confucius would propose and develop the procedures to carry out this undertaking. However, such an interpretation is hardly justifiable if one sticks to the strict literality of the texts. Even if the religious fact transits as a well-known reference, always contemplating a certain propensity to predestination (*Analects*, 2.4) and with respect to spirituality (*Analects* 3.12, 6.20 and 11.11).

On the contrary, these texts show a very different approach of a philosophy with a very strong ethical component immanent to the human condition itself. Confucius' proposal does not derive from any religious dogma, nor does it claim to comply with any of them. Confucius proposes what his rational observation of the world and his profound knowledge of the sources of Chinese knowledge have advised him what he honestly considers most suitable for a better organisation and a better functioning of life. So, he does not base his thinking on implicit religious principles, which he sporadically alludes to as elements that form part of what is common knowledge. It is an approach that can be assumed from perfectly agnostic or even atheistic positions, which is probably where much of its universality lies.

It is true that the *Analects* contain a considerable naturalistic aftertaste. Its texts reveal a conviction, deeply rooted in the Chinese culture of the time, that the cosmos possessed a universal harmony. Among other things, it was responsible for the natural regulation of everything in it: the stars, natural phenomena and their cycles, animals and nature, and human relationships and actions. But if we stick to the strict Confucian text, all this is directly aimed at discussing the last of these sections, the one that has to do with the behaviour of men and, through them, of the societies within which they are inscribed. The rest is taken for granted as context.

In addition, the existence of a Confucian-based religiosity that has survived to the present day is evident. Confucius, the Analects, their content and their legacy are probably an exceptional case in human history. An ethical reflection has ended up becoming a religion, without any theological revelation.

2.3 Confucian Ethics

Confucius' work and his life are an undoubted ethical response to the complex and convulsive times in which he lived. This political breakdown implied a substantial transformation in the perception of society. Without the figure of a king as a guarantor of collective harmony, various centres of power emerged, with their corresponding hegemonic figures and the inevitable clashes between them. It is up to the individual to try to help establish a new balance. Therefore, it is not a question of restoring an old order already lost and closed, but of having it as a reference point in the constitution of a new balanced society; hence the importance of the individual's contribution to this undertaking, which ultimately comes down to ethics. This general and programmatic framework takes the form of very specific virtues (De Prada, 2015).

Thus, the ethical component that articulates Confucius's approaches seems an obvious and immediate response to an exceptional juncture in Chinese history. Of course, it has been unanimously underlined by the literature, which has not hesitated to equate him with Socrates for Western thought, both from the East (Fung Yu-lan, 2005) and from the West (De Prada, 2015). This universality in the Confucian reception is an intrinsic element of his own line of thought, since it advocates the goodness of mankind and projects towards a non-adjectivized ethical horizon (Carlier, 2011). This ethic, moreover, entailed a subtle but substantial transformation of perception. Reclaiming the active and principal participation of man with values in the contemporary world implied shifting the focal point of historical time towards the present (Duranti, 2010: 30).

Concentrating on the present did not imply neglecting the past, given the idyllic and exemplary character attributed to it. So much so that even Confucius himself regarded himself as an interpreter of tradition, rather than the creator of a doctrinal system (Lunyu 7.1). Even he did not hesitate to point to veiled precedents in the Zhou dynasty era. The latter may well be a rhetorical gesture, very much in keeping with the ideal of modesty that he advocates continuously throughout his work.

On the other hand, formulating an ethic was a direct response to a historical conjuncture which, as noted above, was extraordinarily complex, unstable and even problematic. Thus, in the face of the social, cultural and spiritual chaos of his time, the only option for those who claimed to be exemplary was to try to reformulate a new system of constructive values, formulated in the hope of regaining lost stability and order.

In any case, Confucian doctrines were not the only ethical option in the face of such complex political coordinates, which were also socially delicate. In fact, there were two major responses to this historical juncture, which from then on would mark the entire trajectory of Chinese thought. Taoism proposed an inner path of concentration and introspection within the individual, which led to considerable social nihilism. At the opposite extreme, Confucius and his disciples advocated an ethic that would have a direct impact on daily life and ultimately allow for a substantial transformation of society away from the state in which the China of his time found itself (Maspero, 2000; Tagliaferri, 2012). Ultimately, individualism and the search for the essence were set against the community and its construction.

This ethical perspective advocated by Confucius is understood as an immanence of the human condition itself. Insofar as the human condition is susceptible to perfection, there are beings who set out to perfect themselves and choose a path to reach that goal. The horizon to which it leads, the guidelines for following it and the precepts to be fulfilled follow naturally and immediately, by the very logic of the objective pursued. Only those options that contribute to improving the world and its inhabitants, to making it fairer, more equitable, orderly and balanced, more easily inhabitable by all those who are part of it, are admissible. Anything else is not only outside their interests but also deserves their reprobation, without hesitation or ambiguity.

2.4 Life as a Path: The "junzi"

In this way, ethics conceived in such terms allows the development of the inner potentialities of the Human Being and proceeds in a progressive way, as a path that perfects it, through skills grouped around two main nuclei: Li and Ren. Li is a part of the self with correction, in an external and social sense on the one hand, and in an intimate and personal sense on the other. Therefore, correctness acts as a principle that governs every facet of life, whether in the material or spiritual order. It includes not only the rituals, the appropriate etiquette for each occasion and the relevant ceremonies but also the learned good manners, the inner discipline and the will to persevere on this path of perfection. By cultivating Li, the conglomerate of virtue that identifies the Ren is developed. In principle, this corresponds to benevolence in a new, broader sense. It is basically a matter of possessing good feelings towards life in general, and concretely towards other people, as well as exercising them, starting with one's own immediate family. Ren acts as an expansive engine from which other virtues, no less decisive for social life, emerge: Zhong, loyalty; Shu, compassionate fidelity and Yi, justice based on good principles. Therefore, existence is determined by the achievements made in this direction, achievements which will be the lasting memory of the passage through the world of men.

The one able to combine all these attributes acquires the status of Junzi, which in Western languages has been translated as "Superior Man", although nowadays it is preferably interpreted as "Kindly Man". The Junzi embodies the ideal model towards which this ethic should be directed and, thematically, he places the real centre around which the Analects revolves. De Prada (2015: 58–60) insists on the delicacy of its translation into Western languages and reviews some of the options adopted in this sense: "gentleman", "good man", "superior man" or "noble man", as opposed to 小 人, xiǎo, "little man", "vile man". This is a term already used in the Chinese tradition, to which Confucius adds a new meaning. He dwells particularly on the Confucian "nobleman", who is not a nobleman by heraldic inheritance, but a condition acquired through education. Moreover, he considers the latter meaning to be particularly relevant at the time it occurs, during the Zhou dynasty, during the decomposition of the traditional feudal order in China up to that time (De Prada, 2015: 60).

In any case, the original terminology evokes times before Confucius, when it was used to designate noble knights, as opposed to the Shumin, the commoners. The new meaning given to it by Confucius is of strict ethical and moral sense. Nevertheless, it has a nuance full of evocations, certainly revealing one of the most deep-rooted concerns of the master of Lu, namely his concern to be able to approach the past, which he feels is much more exemplary than his own time. It is necessary to follow the example of the ancient sovereigns to be enlightened by the Odes inherited, thanks to tradition to maintain the good ancestral customs. So, this reference to the figure of the Junzi to personify his ethical ideal is completely symptomatic and relevant.

To achieve this moral and ethical state, Confucius recommends the practice of five great virtues (Yao, 2000; Zhenjiang, 2014). This list starts from 文, wén, "language" or "writing", in a general sense, which is extended to "the arts of peace", "of culture", as opposed to those of war. Through them, or thanks to their practice, anyone becomes 君, jūnzǐ. The perfection of oneself, the acquisition and development of culture, acquires a civilising projection through the attainment of more morally exemplary individuals. The second virtue is represented by the character 恕, shù, for which a first translation is proposed as "forgiving", although it is immediately extended to "indulgence" or "reciprocity" (in the sense of not doing to others what one does not want for oneself). The character 德 "dé" introduces the third great Confucian virtue, now interpreted as "moral", and once again, reinterpreted as "power" (of the example given to others).

The next Confucian virtue 孝, "xiao", refers to "filial piety", one of the key concepts in the Confucian conceptual universe. It refers, of course, to the care and attention given by children to their parents. It also establishes a network of immediate social ties of enormous magnitude and depth: parents and children, husbands and wives, older children and younger children, older friends and younger friends and rulers and subjects.

Finally, with 禮, "li", the list of moral tools that make it possible to achieve the state of 君子 jūnzǐ, a term that has been almost unanimously translated as "rite" in all European languages from the 18th century to the present day, comes to an end. In any case, De Prada (2015: 62) notes that Confucius resorts to a conception of rite, rather than as a collective ceremonial manifestation, as a procedure of inner discipline.

This sum of virtues will allow this new Junzi to be in the Just Middle theory, a point of perfect balance that makes him conduct himself by means of moderation without extenuations or nuances in all his vital facets. Therefore, the aim is to train citizens capable of conducting themselves by means of this parameter, the golden mean, as a guarantor of social harmony.

The status of Junzi, of Noble Man or Good Human Being, marks the apex of an itinerary of inner perfection, which is only within the reach of a few who can crown it. They are naturally contrasted with much of the population, the Xiaoren, who lack these virtues and this degree of perfection. Such a pronounced dichotomy may lead to interpret the configuration of the Junzi group in quasi-caste terms. It is a temptation, perhaps justifiable by appearances, but certainly not justified by the profound reality of the Analects. The status of the Noble Man is attained through training, modesty, constancy; it is not an inherited condition that is carried from birth and exercised without much individual perseverance. The instruments for that are basically two, and they are mutually implied: study and introspection. The former leads to the latter; the latter deepens the former. These are the prerequisites for attaining this status of a "good man", which is therefore devoid of any form of external conditioning. Anyone can attain it through the appropriate procedures.

2.5 Education

To tread this path, it was essential to acquire education, the right and accurate training. On this point Confucius followed a universal procedure that is almost constant in any place and any culture. All ethics must be projected in formative actions on the population at which it is aimed. A different being, a new citizen, needs the relevant training to acquire this new mentality and perspective. That was a conviction shared by the other members of the School of Lawyers, all of whom were specifically involved not only as teachers and trainers but also in establishing the parameters within which this training process was to be conducted.

Confucius is deeply suspicious of natural intuitive knowledge. On the contrary, he recommends systematic study based on the imitation of the solvent masters, always depositaries of the knowledge inherited from the past. Only learning has to be carefully weighted by reflection, the guarantor of the internalisation of knowledge.

In any case, the Confucian model of education is developed through the six arts—ritual, music, archery, cart riding, calligraphy and arithmetic—and has as its great common goal the development of morally upright citizens. To this end, he is as concise as possible, trying to make his disciples think. The Book of Odes, a compendium of beauty and exemplarity, occupies an absolutely central place in the educational process, repeatedly referred to in the Analects. Confucius considers them an inescapable point of reference for the moral development of the individual.

Of course, Lu's teacher seems to have been involved in this task since he figures as one of the great persons responsible for the configuration of the educational canon known as the *Five Classics*. That was a corpus that became a fundamental element in the history of China. *The Yijing*, translated into Western languages as the Book of Mutations, dealt with changes. It was basically a divinatory manual, probably shaped around the 11th century B.C. The *Shujing*, or *Book of History* contains ancient historical documentation, including alleged texts of rulers from the Xia dynasty onwards. It also contains a variety of historical materials, including official documents and conversations between rulers. It is also a source for knowledge of everyday life in ancient times, with many commentaries on the legal system, education and major patterns of thought. Thirdly, the *Shījīng, Book of Odes or Book of Poetry* contains 305 ancient compositions including 160 folk songs, 74 works for court festivities, 31 pieces performed at solemn ceremonies and 40 hymns from the rites performed in the royal household. *The Lǐjing*, or *Record of Ritual* is a monographic work on this subject compiling social and etiquette rules and ceremonials from the Zhou dynasty. Finally, the *Chūnqiū*, the *Spring and Autumn Annals* is another historical work, this time covering feudal China from the 8th century B.C. to the death of Confucius.

Traditionally, the authorship of all of them had been attributed to Confucius himself, although more recent historiography has cast serious doubt on this (Chin, 2007; Jin-Bo, 2008; Vogelsgang, 2010). It is to some extent a secondary consideration to determine the exact authorship, if possible, in view of the repercussions it acquired over a very long period. These fragments were teaching texts from 136 B.C. until practically the 20th century. They even became the subject of examinations for access to the civil service.

This educational path, which lies at the heart of the Confucian ethical system, has more than direct repercussions on the personality of the individual. Everything revolves around the idea of "ren", understood as "compassion" or "love for others", with the consequent renunciation of part of oneself. Thus, it introduces a strong emphasis on the social dimension of personal identity. That had a number of practical consequences that sought to avoid or encourage certain behaviours. On the negative side, it was necessary to avoid elaborate discourse and anything that implied arrogance or presumption. At the other end, the cultivation of the renegade encouraged the necessary modesty to put oneself at the service of others. This pattern of social behaviour becomes a spider's web that extends progressively from the family, the nuclear unit in Confucius' conception, and the source of harmony beyond it. In this sense, it underlines the link that is maintained across generations and over time, whereby the individual was directly linked to his ancestors and successors. From that axis, the individual played other social roles outside the extended family: among his neighbours, in the administration of the state and politics.

Of course, none of these virtues are acquired naturally. It is men who must persevere to acquire them and become a good citizen, a circumstance that ultimately gives meaning to the idea of the path as a progressive itinerary of personal deepening and improvement (Cheng, 1997: 60–61).

2.6 Ritual

This progressive perfection is gathered in the emblematic image of the "Path" that the individual must follow until he reaches the perfection of the Noble (Superior) Man, who is above all a Good Man, in what constitutes one of the main signs of identity of Confucian thinking. This entails the consequent discipline and self-control that are essential to follow this path steadily and without deviation from it.

One of the main instruments for achieving this objective lies in the ritual, the li, another inexcusable reference in his thought which must be carefully qualified. The li is not the exclusive guarantor of Confucian righteousness. It is a valuable and essential element, insofar as it formalises decorum and respect in a bidirectional sense. On the one hand, it is the respect that the individual must show towards others. On the other hand, it is also the respect that he must receive from them.

Therefore, from the Confucian point of view it is not limited to a set of repetitive and empty practices. On the contrary, Confucius advocates a ritual understood as an effective experience, oriented towards inner perfection and a manifestation of the will to contribute to collective cohesion. In this sense, it is not a monasticism that implies drastic renunciations of life, but a way of conducting them. It is not in vain that he is convinced that through the rite an inner improvement of the person is achieved.

Although this understanding of ritual is partly linked to traditional religious practices, it is also clear that Confucius transcends them. It does so above all by conceiving the rite, rather than as an activity, repetitively and with the risk of being ultimately empty of content, as an attitude and as an experience on the part of the person who participates in it. Hence, ultimately, this conception admits a secular reading, insofar as it establishes forms and principles of behaviour, with an evident social vocation from the very outset. Above all, it is a privileged opportunity to practise self-discipline, the exercise of the personal will to abide by certain principles, as well as to follow them constantly and strictly.

As mentioned above, there is no shortage of people who have linked it to the professional practice of the Rújiā (De Prada, 2015). Indeed, these seem to have been the descendants of an ancient class specialised in the elaboration and application of rites, not unrelated to magical practices or the invocation of the forces of nature. However, this figure disappeared, and by the time of Confucius, it had become a class of teachers who lived by transmitting their knowledge in an itinerant way. To return to the figure of the rite is, as on so many other occasions, a way of linking up with that formally longed-for past. But, as in other cases, its content is ostensibly different, as discussed here. Hence, this new meaning of the rite acts as a powerful symbol in Confucian semiotics, given that it is capable of amalgamating and linking times, until it finds a line of continuity that, at the same time, inaugurates a new time, based on the order between the elements of life and the sequence in which they are produced in it.

Moreover, the rite has a second dimension, the social one, which partly derives from the individual aspect discussed so far. Confucius holds the firm conviction that good ceremonial application promotes the proper governance of the state. On the one hand, ritual externalises the social status attained by an individual or, potentially, a family. Not everyone has access to the same rites, so it is a way of manifesting that status. On the other hand, it acts as a unifying factor that gives coherence to the social dynamic itself. There are no exceptions to the observance of ritual, not even for rulers, who must be subject to it, like any other citizen. Therefore, they constitute a parameter of social formalisation and even a supervisory element that affects all citizens indiscriminately. Those who do not comply with the rite, including kings, are not worthy of the social place they occupy. Indeed, power is not omnipotent, but it is limited by the guidelines imposed by higher ethics, externalised through rituals.

2.7 The Organisation of Society

For Confucius, the Noble Men, given their ethical stature, should be in charge of the management of society since they are the ones who have reached the highest degree of perfection among their fellow men. Of course, it ties in with an old and well-known recommendation of Chinese thought, as discussed. In any case, he manages to make it explicit and systematise it in his own specific way. Therein lies another of the constants of his school of thought. His ethics does not have a personal finalist objective. It is not enough for the individual to improve, or even to achieve perfection for perfection's sake. This must be projected towards the improvement of the society of which he is a part, always guiding it in the right direction. The individual is only conceivable in the heart of a society, for which progressive improvement the Noble Men work, in what was naturally one of the core precepts of the *Rújiā*.

This leads to a pyramid-shaped society structured around the individual, the family and the state. The individual is part of a family, conceived in much more extensive terms than will be the case in the Judeo-Christian tradition. The Chinese family of which Confucius speaks is a broad unit, composed of relatives beyond parental-filial relations, even sharing physical space, amalgamated around a common ancestor whom they share and revere. In fact, such a family functions as a small state and ultimately establishes a dialectical link with it. If individuals make families function in an exemplary way, the state will end up behaving in the same way. Vice versa, when the state is governed by the right principles, its example is transmitted to the family units and, within these, to the individuals who compose them. Between the state and the family there are a significant number of intermediate strata: vassals to lords and nobles, civil servants, the court. But, as in the case of the label Noble Man, the similarity with the old Chinese feudal society is more an evocation, a nomenclature and a relatively profound aftertaste than a tangible and effective reality. In fact, the proposal of the Confucian School of the Learned is considerably subversive in its time, precisely because of the requirements for attaining that ultimate wisdom that adorns the Noble Man. None. There are no prerequisites; anyone can attain it if they have enough will to set out in that direction and persevere in it. Therefore, there are no privileges of birth, which at the same time makes it likely that anyone who departs from the straight path is liable to be criticised, wherever they come from. Certainly, the Analects leave ample evidence of this attitude, with abundant censure of the behaviour of important people, nobles and even rulers. Confucius was consistent in his thinking, formally opposing the court of Lu and abandoning his public offices, as previously discussed.

To such an extent must rulers be subject to Confucius' moral imperatives that even they are not exempt from rituals, another of the constants of the Analects and the thought of the *Rújiā*.

Like his whole thought, Confucius' political conception does not avoid exemplarity. The good ruler is the one who can display it, for which he needs to be educated, to persevere in study, to submit to internal discipline and to be virtuous, just like any other citizen who intends to follow the right path. This political ideal is openly at odds with his time, which is far removed from these parameters in the performance of political responsibilities.

2.8 Language as an Instrument of Civilisation

Language is one of the main tools available to fulfil these political tasks. So, it becomes a necessary component to complete the patterns of proper civilisation.

To begin with, Confucius shows a clear awareness about the role language can play in maintaining social and political order (Lonobile, 2012: 11; Lu, 2004: 31–32), primarily due to its performative capacity (Cheng, 1997: 68–70). Put in such general terms not much can be objected to either. But, for a linguist, it is an imprecise statement in some ways. Confucius is not thinking of just any facet of human language, not even of a particular language, but of a very specific area concerning the public and social uses of language. From this conceptual core, several consequences can be derived, more diversified on the one hand and not as hermetic as has sometimes been suggested in the literature on the other. It has even been claimed that Confucius thinks of language as a prescriptive element of behaviour (Lonobile, 2012: 25) so that any social activity is previously established and regulated, based on specific and prescribed verbal uses.

However, a more leisurely reading of the Analects does not invite us to think of a dogmatic and prescriptive order, neither in relation to language nor in relation to any other aspect. Confucius proposes a series of principles aimed at restoring coherence to a world in chaos.

This coherence begins with names designating what they really are and mean. The correctness of names, by the way, is not an exclusive concern of Confucius, but one of the great questions running through the Chinese thought at the time. This requirement, the correctness of names, naturally becomes an inexcusable element to govern (Marinelli, 2009: 2–3). But, at the same time, it transcends this political dimension, because the correctness of names is, first and foremost, a question of the adequacy of things. Concretely, it deals with the ways in which they manifest themselves in accordance with their nature. Therefore, language becomes a product of rationality for the interpretation of the world, as in Plato (Romaniello, 2004: 11).

In that way, a kind of conceptual succession is established, as Siary and Vergnaud (1993: 66) point out: to act well means to govern well, for which it is necessary to say well and write well. Ultimately, Confucius' position is a response to a crisis of behaviour (doing well) and social interrelation (saying well) that were manifested in China from the 8th to the 5th century B.C. There is a dialectical link between these elements. It is not enough to say correctly, but it is necessary to act correctly, to support what is said. In the same way, the correct use of names is essential for the exemplarity of actions; verbal behaviour is worthless when it is not corroborated by the corresponding correct actions.

From this macro-function of language arise more specific tasks that affect various facets and components of verbal activity. Confucius constructs an authentic rhetorical system (Oliver, 1971) which maintains a line of continuity within Chinese culture. His rhetorical canon begins in the 8th century B.C., with the references of poetry (Shi Jing, 诗经) or history (Shu Jing, 书经). The *Analects* (Lunyu, 论语) follow the ethical and epistemological emphasis of these texts (Lonobile, 2012: 20–21).

On the other hand, it underlines the truth value of the written word, a fundamental tool for the development of the administrative activity performed by political action (Duranti, 2010: 23). Moreover, this function is universally associated with writing since its very appearance as a human skill, both in China and Mesopotamia (García Marcos, 2009).

Finally, as will be developed in the following chapters, Confucius is very attentive to the communicative behaviour of people from an ethical point of view. The way a person verbally acts is a transcriber of ethical principles, but also, and simultaneously, constitutes an ethical action. One speaks and writes in a certain way when one has the corresponding ethical basis for doing so. In the same way, using the appropriate language at each moment and in each situation is a way of continuing the intellectual and human journey that lies at the heart of the Analects. So much so that the Confucian Noble Man, or the good man, is distinguished by verbal behaviour in accordance with his ethical principles. In the same way that he is exemplary in his actions, in his attitudes and in his disposition, he continues to be exemplary in his use of language.

References

Barreno, P. G. (2017). La Academia «Chi-hsia» o «Jixia». *Boletín de la Real Academia Española, 97*(315), 257-265.

Carlier, D. (2011). Un regard sur Confucius. *Sens public.* https://doi.org/10.7202/1063067ar (Access: 26-12-2017).

Cheng, A. (1997). Storia del pensiero cinese - Volume primo. Torino: Einaudi [ed. originale: Histoire de la pensée chinoise, trad. di Amina Crisma].

Chin, A. (2007). *The authentic Confucius: A life of thought and politics.* New York: Scribner.

———. (2009). *Confucius: A life of thought and politics.* Yale: Yale University Press.

De Beaugrande, R. (2011). Text linguistics. In J. Zienkowski et al. (Eds.), *Handbook of Pragmatics Highlights (HoPH).* Amsterdam: Benjamins, 286-298.

De Beaugrande, R. A., & Dressler, W. U. (1981). *Introduction to text linguistics* (Vol. 1). London: Longman.

De Prada García, A. (2015). Confucio y la escuela de los letrados: humanidad y armonía. *La Albolafia: Revista de Humanidades y Cultura,* (4), 51-64.

Duranti, M. (2010). *La concezione della storia in Li Dazhao.* Roma: Aracne.

Foltz, P. W., Kintsch, W., & Landauer, T. K. (1998). The measurement of textual coherence with latent semantic analysis. *Discourse Processes, 25*(2-3), 285-307.

García Marcos, F. (2009). *Aspectos de historia social de la lingüística.* Barcelona: Octaedro.

Halliday, M. A. K., & Webster, J. J. (2014). *Text linguistics: The how and why of meaning.* Sheffield: Equinox.

Jin-bo, N. I. (2008). Two discussions on biography of Confucius of historical records. *Journal of Weinan Teachers University, 6.* 257-265.

Levi, J. (2012). *Confucius.* Paris: Pygmalion.

———. (2018). Les assassins de Confucius. Du négationnisme dans la sinologie américaine contemporaine. 2018. halshs-01881797 (Access: 26-12-2017).

Lu, X. (2004). *Rhetoric of the Chinese cultural revolution: The impact on Chinese thought, culture and communication.* Columbia: University of South Carolina Press.

Marinelli, M. (2009). Names and reality in Mao Zedong's political discourse on intellectuals. *Journal of Global Cultural Studies, 5,* 1-31.

Maspero, H. (2000). *El taoísmo y las religiones chinas.* Barcelona: Trotta.

Oliver, R. T. (1971). *Communication and culture in ancient India and China.* New York: University of Siracusse Press.

Prevosti i Monclús, A.; Del Río, A. and N. Prats, Ramon. (2014). Pensamiento y religión en Asia Oriental. Barcelona; Editorial UOC.

Roberts, J. A. (2011). *A history of China*. London: Palgrave/Macmillan International Higher Education.

Romaniello, G. (2004). *Pensiero e linguaggio: grammatica universale*. Roma: Sovera Edizioni.

Sarkissian, H. (2010). Confucius and the effortless life of virtue. History of Philosophy Quarterly, 27(1), 1-16.

Shih, I. (1970). The place of Confucius in the History of Chinese religion: A tentative interpretation. *Gregorianum*, 51, 3: 485-508.

Siary, G., & Vergnaud, F. (2009). Quand faire, c'est dire: Confucius et la *Rectitude des noms*, *Cahiers de praxématique*, 20 (http://journals.openedition.org/praxematique/171). (Access: 26-12-2017).

Smith, D. H. (1963). The significance of Confucius for Religion. *History of Religions*, *2*(2), 242-255.

Tagliaferri, A. (2012). *Il taoismo*. Roma: Newton Compton Editori.

Tierney, R. J., & Mosenthal, J. H. (1983). Cohesion and textual coherence. *Research in the Teaching of English*, 17, 3: 215-229.

Vogelsang, K. (2010). Beyond Confucius: A Socio-historical Reading of the "Lunyu". *Oriens Extremus*, *49*, 29-61.

Wilson, T. A. (Ed.). (2020). *On sacred grounds: Culture, society, politics, and the formation of the cult of Confucius*. Cambridge: Harvard University Press.

Yao, X. (2000). *El confucianismo* (Vol. 10). Madrid: AKAL, 2001.

Zhenjiang, Z. (2014). Confucio, ética y civilización. *Co-herencia*, *11*(20), 165-178.

3

Confucian Man's Ways of Communicating

Communication is present in all the sections of the scheme with which Confucius structures the *Analects*. It is part of Li, insofar as it expresses the necessary correctness of human activities, as well as being subject to it. The form of the rites' language cannot be just any old form, just as etiquette. The proper forms for correct social relations require an adequate and pertinent verbalisation. This double dimension of everything linked to communicative interaction through verbal language, as agent and recipient, is also present in Ren. It must be linked to—and governed by—the benevolence and weighting that the Righteous Middle demands. Likewise, kind words and fair terms are the corresponding ways of exercising both.

Therefore, communication becomes one of the greatest cross-cutting concerns of the Analects. All ethics aspires by its nature to be communicated as efficiently as possible. Otherwise, when communication is neglected or even omitted, ethics loses much of its raison d'être, the main purpose for which it was developed. Moreover, ethics must also necessarily consider a factor such as communication. That is crucial in terms of formalising the human relations on which it intends to act. So, dealing with communication is an imperative for these interests, but also a requirement for its success. It depends on the communicative effectiveness that can develop.

In turn, all this refers to a deeper question about the societal nature of the Human Being, to which Confucius is no stranger. Communication occupies an absolutely central place in the development of the species even from a biological point of view. It is a fact that palaeontologists have long insisted on. In a classic work in this field, Maturana and Varela (1984) explain how the differential evolution of the human species is directly linked to the development of a more complex communicative capacity than that of other animals.

Of course, the societal nature of language, and the implications of this for the development of life, has been a constant and universal concern among humans. So much so that when scientific procedures had not yet been developed to describe and explain it, myths were invoked early on to address this concern. The first of these—and probably also the most frequently referred to—was that of the Tower of Babel, as it appears first in the *Book of Genesis* (11: 1–9) and later in the *Book of Jubilees* (10: 20–21). In their pride, men begin to build a tower to reach the heights where God is supposed to dwell in the plain of Senaar. To undo this foolish claim, the divinity infuses the builders with different languages, making it impossible to continue the work and the endeavour. In the first instance, Babel addresses another concern as universal in human history as linguistic diversity. It is God who is responsible for its existence, among other things, to teach men a lesson. In addition, the myth addresses the role played by language in the articulation of society. Without an efficient mechanism of communication, the great human work declines to the point of becoming unviable. What is interesting is that this is not a figure exclusive to the *Old Testament*. In fact, the myth of Babel comes from the Mesopotamian imagination. Some authors have even identified it with the temple of Etemenanki, built in the 4th century B.C. in honour of Marduk, the main deity of the Mesopotamian world (Harris, 2002). In any case, there is a more direct Sumerian precedent in the story of Emmerkar, king of Uruk, who initiates the construction of a castle at Eridu. However, at a certain point he invokes the god Enki to spread linguistic diversity in the world, whereupon the construction is interrupted (Kramer, 1968; Liverani, 2008). After the *Old Testament* it will be taken up again, both in authors such as Pseudo-Philon (circa 70), Flavius Josephus (circa 30–70) or Baruch (2nd century), as well as in rabbinic literature. It is thus a widespread concern that has been answered since ancient times.

Therefore, addressing communication implies delving into truly core aspects of the human condition, inexcusable for an ethical perspective. Confucius responds to this imperative in an ample and solvent manner, which is yet another universal feature of his legacy.

3.1 The Quantitative Weight of Communication

This communicative concern takes on different manifestations in the *Analects*. Sometimes it deals with its forms, sometimes with the precepts that govern it or with its development in various spheres of social formality; in any case, it never loses track of the perceptible influence it maintains on the ethical formation of individuals. The latter is the reason for its regular and constant presence through-out the development of the work. It is not a trivial issue, but appears as one of the decisive tools to orientate oneself on the right path, the one that ensures the devel-opment of the virtuous capacities that correspond to the talent and performance of the Noble Man. This perception can even be quantifiable evidence, as Table 3.1 shows. The Analects are made up of twenty books, subdivided internally into chapters of varying number in each of them. The table specifies for each book the number of chapters in which Confucius is concerned with an issue related to communication, together with the total number of chapters in each book in question.

Table 3.1. Headings with communication-related content in the *Analects* of Confucius

Book	Com.	Tot.	%
I	8	16	50.0
II	4	24	16.6
III	4	26	15.3
IV	3	26	11.5
V	7	7	25.9
VI	3	28	10.7
VII	4	37	10.8
VIII	4	1	19.0
IX	3	30	10.0
X	6	18	33.3
XI	8	25	32.0
XII	8	24	33.3
XIII	8	30	26.6
XIV	12	47	25.5
XV	16	41	39.0
XVI	12	14	85.7
XVII	9	26	34.6
XVIII	2	11	18.1

Book	Com.	Tot.	%
XIX	5	25	20.0
XX	3	3	100.0

Book; Com. = Chapters dealing with the theme of communication; Tot. = Total

There is no lack of references to communication in any of the chapters of the book. More than half of them, twelve to be precise, have communicative content in more than 20% of their headings. At the lowest extreme, communication is never present in less than 10% of a chapter, and at the other extreme, three chapters contain more than 50%, with the last one being the absolute maximum. In fact, the work concludes with a reflection on language and on its capital importance for understanding the true and deepest human nature.

Figure 3.1 illustrates what is being discussed. It is true that some chapters seem more monographically concentrated on communication. But, as it can be seen, it has a regular and continuous presence in the work as a whole.

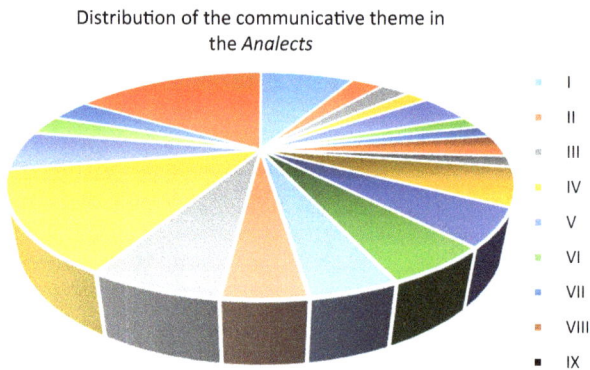

Figure 3.1. Distribution of the communicative theme in the *Analects*

Thus, from a mere quantitative approach, communication is a very significant constant in the plot and development of the Analects, which transcribes the importance Confucius attaches to this issue.

3.2 Harmful Communication

Numbers offer a formalised approximation of reality. But they are hardly capable of explaining it in its depth. In the Analects there are many nuances related to communication—many details, of different depth and scope, which certainly escape the brief reflection of the figures.

As in other aspects of his ethical proposal, the Analects take stock of both the dangers and the benefits of communicative activity. Naturally, it is extended in the last of them. Its ultimate purpose is to show the right path, those precepts and habits of life that should lead to exemplary social behaviour. But neither does he neglect the obverse side of this model of correctness, the negative side of the scale in terms of the ways of interacting verbally with others which, consequently, must be prevented. His list of dangers to be avoided in relation to communication is quite explicit.

3.2.1 Rhetoric and Grandiloquence

Undoubtedly, verbal grandiloquence and haughtiness constitute one of the main Confucian concerns about the social uses of languages. More than a relatively one-off issue, they form a thematic block to which other neighbouring verbal vices such as flattery or arrogance are associated.

Good words should not be confused with the words of the good ones. The virtuous need not necessarily conduct themselves by means of exclusively good words (XIV–V: 126). Sometimes they must express themselves forcefully in the face of situations, actions or persons who deviate from the straight path. Confucian virtue does not envisage unlimited condescension. On the contrary, it presupposes a firm set of principles and rigorous opposition to anything that deviates from them. Therefore, politely opposing stubborn deviations from that direction, even remaining silent, is part of what is permissible for those who claim to be virtuous. The Noble Man, for example, must not lie to others about what his true capacities are (XIX–XIII: 161).[9]

In the same way, not all words that are good in appearance are good in substance. This is a recurring theme in the *Analects*. Confucius repeatedly warns of the dangers, in his opinion, of clever verbs (XV–XVI: 139), insinuating statements and appearances (XVI–XVIII: 152), fine words with a benevolent countenance

---

9 From now on, the book number, chapter number and pages of the Spanish edition used here will be cited.

(I–III: 51), sumptuous linguistic formulas (V–XXIV: 75) and sweetened criticisms (VI–XIV: 79); all of them show behaviours contrary to the right path of virtue, which can be seriously misleading. Their use is at odds with benevolence and can even become a cause for embarrassment, like complacent countenance or excessive politeness. The latter was an idea of Zuo Qiuming's[10] which Confucius shared (V–XXIV: 75). Thus, he considers all forms of eloquence unnecessary. It is possible to become virtuous, like Yong, by dispensing with verbal excesses, which has the added benefit of avoiding being hated (V–IV: 71). Naturally, such linguistic behaviour is counterproductive for social life, to the extent that he is convinced that for the exemplary government of a country it is essential to avoid the danger posed by those who express themselves through sophistry (XV–X: 137).

3.2.2 Other Vices Stemming from Rhetoric

Rhetoric is immediately associated with other no less counterproductive uses of language, largely because of it, directly or indirectly. In the first place, flattery is to be avoided under all circumstances. There are no extenuating circumstances, not even for the poor, in whom it is not seen as necessary. Instead, he prefers them to be happy in their humility (I–XV: 54). In his creed there is a starting point located in the personal coherence of everyone, only point from which it is possible to begin that path of perfection to which every individual can aspire. Consequently, this coherent assumption of what each person is does not allow for regrets or complaints. To do so is to avoid self-awareness and lose the references from which to perfect oneself.

So notorious is his dislike of flattery that he considers friendship with those who practise it systematically to be harmful (XVI–IV: 144). Flattery misrepresents sincere relationships, which should be manifested through transparent and direct procedures. In the same way, he dislikes the arrogance of those who think they are able to find an answer to everything (XI–XIV: 110). That is basically the antipodes of his conception of a virtuous person, as an individual in

10 Zuo Qiuming was an author of the Lu court and a contemporary of Confucius. He seems to have authored the Zuo Zhuan, a historical text, and is credited with being involved in the Guo Yu, another historical work covering the Zhou to the Qin dynasty. Traditionally, it has been noted that he lost his sight. In any case, he must have been an authoritative figure for Confucius. In fact, he quotes him on another occasion, in the same *Analects,* when referring to his criticism of people who feign friendship, when deep down they experience resentment.

permanent search and, consequently, in a continuous process of learning from the masters, from the ancients, Odes and traditions. One can only learn from the modesty of those who are willing to listen, to learn from what they have heard and to put what they have learned into practice.

3.2.3 *Lies, Falsehoods, Slander*

However, the only danger in the use of language does not only come from artificial refinement. There are other forms, much more daily life and commonplace, which are no less pernicious. Among them, Confucius is particularly concerned about backbiting, slander and lying. To be oblivious to gossip or to accusations is a sign of intellectual acuity for Confucius (XII–VI: 113). It is also a sign of prudence, insofar as frequent criticism always leads to disgrace, whether in the service of the prince or in mere friendship, as he puts it in the mouth of Ziyou (IV–XXVI: 70). This is not just any reference. Ziyou (or Yan, Yanzí)[11] is one of the most prominent disciples of Confucius, whom he considers especially distinguished in the study of the classics.

He acknowledges that this is neither an easy nor an immediate task. In order to distance oneself from complaints and murmurings, it is necessary to observe a strict personal self-demand, which obliges to decline as little responsibility as possible for fellow men (XV–XIV: 137). Moreover, publishing other people's evils is one of the things that a Noble Man unequivocally rejects (XVII–XIV: 153). Among other things, slander cannot reach those lofty and kind individuals. To Shusun Wushu's insults,[12] Zigong[13] replies that Confucius is so far above them that they simply do not affect him because they do not reach him (XIX–XXIV: 163).

---

11 Forty-five years younger than the master, Ziyou was a native of Wu, where he took up important positions in the administration which he conducted along the lines proposed by Confucius. He received posthumous recognition as a wise man, and today he is still among the Twelve Sages of the Confucian temples. His tablet is placed fourth from the west.

12 High dignitary of the house of Lu, contemporary with Confucius. He belonged to the house of Huan, one of the three hegemonic families of that state.

13 Duanmu Ci, or Zigong in his courtly version, thirty-one years younger than Confucius, a native of Wei. He was one of the most notorious disciples and referred to in the *Analects*. A successful merchant by profession before he met his mentor, he was noted for his readiness and farsightedness in learning. He later rose to positions of responsibility in Lu and Wei. His master was not always pleased with his performance, sometimes complaining about his excessive verbosity and rigidity. In any case, he is also on the list of the Twelve Sages.

However, there are procedures to keep out from these dangers. It is necessary not to abandon oneself to careless speech, making our what we hear from others—or on the roads, as Confucius points out—without further reflection, which is a severe attack on virtue (XVII-XIV: 121). This is not in contradiction to the attentiveness presupposed by the renunciation of modesty. It does introduce a principle of cautious distancing, insofar as it is necessary to weigh up what the individual receives, evaluate it and assess it before accepting it without further ado.

Lying is also reviled, although it does not affect the Noble Man either, whose virtue and preparation make him largely immune to it: he can be lied to, although it is difficult to confuse him (VI-XXIV: 81). In any case, it seems to be an extreme version of slander. Of course, when the lie undermines the social hierarchy, it is much more pernicious. Confronting the princes is considered a serious offence, mainly because of the attack on social order that it entails (XIV, XXIII: 129).

3.2.4 Nuances and Mitigating Factors for Harmful Verbal Habits

The Confucian universe's elaborate web of verbal precepts and rules is not exempt from the possibilities of accommodation, of attenuation even, always under considerably restricted conditions and rather strict precepts. In *Wei Ling Gong*, the fifteenth book of the *Analects,* he seems particularly sensitive to this in two passages. In the first of these (XV-VII: 136) he discusses the relevance of communication between equals. Confucius applies his binary conception of the world to communication, which becomes an extension of it, but at the same time an instrument that nourishes and perpetuates it. Simply put, we must speak to whom we must speak. That is, it is understood that only those who are already on the path of ethical and moral improvement, or those who are able to find and follow it, and vice versa. Those who do not meet these requirements are not worthy of human attention, of disturbing the concentration of the seeker of virtues who, consequently, should not waste conversations on them either. The second accommodation to the interlocutor is much more concrete (XV-XLIII: 142). The Analects tell how Confucius alters part of his communicative routines with the music master Miam (XV-XLIII: 142). He speaks to him differently because he is blind and explains it that way to his disciples. His system of rules, too formal and sober, too strict at times, nevertheless allows for appropriate flexibility in specific and justified cases. This denotes that it is an ethic that accommodates itself to reality and to the human being, not a set of dogmatic principles that must be followed regardless of any circumstance or nuance.

3.3 The Contribution of Communication to the Development of Ethics' Virtue

There a positive side as well. Verbal conduct contributes to building the environment and spirit necessary to the development of virtue. Of course, virtue must be understood in Confucian terms, as an inner discipline and balance that enables the individual to behave constructively towards the society in which he or she lives. In this sense, there are ways of communicating that contribute to this goal, with a double involvement level, personal on the one hand, and collective and social on the other.

The above-mentioned linguistic habits are also negative in these two simultaneous dimensions. If individuals do not find the virtue, the perfection of each one of them, it will be impossible to rebuild a harmonious and an exemplary organised society. At the very least, a part of this population, even if it is a minority, must be able to put these guiding principles into practice. With their example they will guide society in the right direction, always with the ideal reference point of the ancient kingdoms.

It can—and should—use language in the other direction, on the positive path. Confucius perseveres in that latent idea, consubstantial to any ethical approach mentioned above, reserving for communication a determining role in his human and social project.

3.3.1 Verbal Prudence and Restraint

To bring linguistic communication to this end, it is essential to handle with care and prudence the various manifestations of these principles of action. On the other hand, it serves as the basis on which a good number of other verbal actions recommended by Confucius are sustained. As a general rule, we should be careful with words, following the example of the Noble Men (IX, XIV: 53). In any case, this declaration of intentions is as magnanimous in scope as it is evidently indeterminate. Roughly speaking, taking care of words implies activating processes of discourse control, of meticulous and adjusted selection of resources, as adequate as possible to the ends to be obtained from the use of language. However, such a generic principle can accommodate even opposing verbal behaviour. For example, the incendiary politician seeking to dazzle the masses, doctoral students preparing their thesis defence, a priest in a homily or a couple in love on their first date usually monitor their verbal behaviour. In other words, they watch their words. The Confucian meaning is much more precise. This imperative has several immediate consequences within its ethical universe. In the first place, it obliges to be cautious in the use of language, especially while not being completely certain about things. Rather than a manifestation of insecurity, it is a matter of applying a precautionary principle of being cautious in the verbal interactions in which we participate. This automatically means that it is advisable not to be completely open (XIII, III: 118). As on many other occasions, a communicative virtue in Confucius is opposed to one of the vices he criticises. While not being completely certain about things, verbal excess can produce imprecise, uncertain, exaggerated messages. All of them are close, if not to lies, at least to the slander that bothers the master of Lu so much. In the best of cases, they are close to inaccuracy, which is just another way of not sticking to the strict reality of things. Therefore, it is necessary to avoid acting with the lightness that he considers pernicious, and simply stick to what is known with complete certainty.

On the other hand, verbal caution shows the goodness of those who practise it (XII, III: 112). Again, this concept must be interpreted in Confucian terms, this time referring to people who are always respectful, without distinction. Any interlocutor, without exception, is worthy of this form of Confucian kindness regardless of their social affiliation.

Verbal caution appears to be connected with another of the main protagonists of this ethical and communicative universe: respect. In fact, this is one of the great civic virtues that Confucius thinks of and has a corresponding verbal component. According to the Confucian perspective, the perfect civic virtue contemplates three indispensable elements: the loyalty that must govern the relationship with others, the respect that must be present in all business-related activities and politeness, even in the most intimate and private relationships (XIII, XIX: 122).

Again, following on from what was referred (XX, II: 166), verbal and ethical respect is observed without distinction, in a generalised manner for all kinds of people. There is no principle of contradiction with the evident hierarchical stratification of society which is insistently advocated in the Analects. Every person deserves respect, intrinsic and consubstantial, regardless of his or her place in this pyramidal framework. From the prince to the humblest villager, they must be worthy of the observance of this principle; they must be the recipients of the greatest possible verbal respect. The society in which Confucius thinks is stratified in the social, as an organising principle, but not in the intrinsic essence of the individuals. Only perseverance in training, in the Way of inner perfection, will end up differentiating them. Moreover, Confucian social stratification does not amount to a diminution or loss of the dignity to which all are entitled. Moreover, in the moral order the differences between members of a society are attributable to the degree of perseverance in virtuous training, not to social origins.

3.3.2 From Verbal Economy to Absolute Silence

Virtuous respect manifests itself precisely by economising as much as possible, both public actions and their verbal component. Verbal economy is an expression, and at the same time an agent, of a model of life: the ideal citizen hears and sees a lot, but only selects what suits him to improve himself as a person (VII, XXVII: 85). Disregarding this precaution can lead to one of the most pernicious effects of harmful communication discussed above: not discriminating everything we hear, the good from the bad, with the consequent risk of misjudging and misunderstanding things, which will result in pernicious verbal behaviour, because it is unfounded and causes confusion among the interlocutors.

Confucius himself expresses prudence and restraint, not only in the Analects as a whole but also in specific passages of them. It is not in vain that he proposes to sum up the 305 odes of the ever-present and pondered *Book of Poetry* in a single brief sentence: "It contains not a single evil thought" (III, III: 55). Thus, he ponders figures such as Zong You[14] and Ran Qiu,[15] whom he avoids regarding as great ministers. Instead, he emphasises that they are just simple and humble officials who have scrupulously fulfilled their duty of describing the surrounding reality in an adequate and considered manner (XI, XXIII: 110).

They will not be the only cases of exemplary persons characterised by their verbal parsimony. The Analects contain an estimable list of similar cases which ultimately show how this is one of the defining characteristics of the Noble Man. That ideal is embodied by Min Sun,[16] a man who speaks little, but when he does,

14 Zhong You (542–480 B.C.), also a native of Lu, was one of Confucius' leading disciples, who rose to positions of responsibility at the courts of Lu and Wei, where he was murdered in a macabre manner. Confucius included him among his twenty-four models of filial piety.

15 Ran Qiu (6th B.C.) was another outstanding disciple of Confucius, this time an expert in military arts. Commander of the Lu army, he achieved very important victories which, among other things, allowed the master to return to his native state after fourteen years of exile. They did not always agree, and Confucius was severely criticised for his dislike of rites and his interest in administration. Nevertheless, he is still regarded as one of his main disciples.

16 Min Sun, or Min Ziqian, was a reputed disciple of Confucius, especially renowned for his moral purity and filial piety. He is listed in Confucian temples in the first

he always gets it right, focused on the issues that need to be addressed specifically and concretely (XI, XIII: 108).

The Noble Man, of impeccable ethics, profound knowledge and integrity, does not need verbal excesses. That is why he avoids unnecessary explanations and limits himself to describing things as they are (XVI, I: 143). He loves simplicity and practises study to avoid coarseness (XVI, VIII: 150) and is capable of restraining himself in the face of the miseries he has to suffer (XV, I: 135). He also conveys profound thoughts in a synthetic and condensed manner, like Boyu[17] when he clarifies three issues to Chen Kang[18] by answering a single question (XVI, XIII: 146). Zay Yu[19] settled disputes continuously, in a fair and even-handed manner, although he hardly needed half a word to do so (XII, XIII: 115). Such is the verbal parsimony advocated in the Analects that the Noble Man zealously limits conversations with his own sons to the maximum, to the point of restricting them to guiding them only in the appropriate readings to follow a proper education and in accordance with a straight path (XVI, XIII: 146).

This limited use of verbal resources is compensated for by the actions that the Noble Man is able to carry out. At times, it might be perceived that Confucius is hesitant about such idiomatic economy, or whether, deep down, it risks being counterproductive, bordering dangerously on incommunicativeness. Only the fear of overdoing it with words is outweighed by the edifying force of congruent and constructive actions (XIV, XXX: 130).

The ideal person in the Confucian social perspective tries to avoid verbal ostentation, one of the most pernicious dangers to correct morals coming from the use of language, as discussed above (XIII, VIII: 120). The Analects even have

place in the east, among the Twelve Sages, after the Four Evaluators. A native of Lu, he is credited with a childhood of abuse at the hands of his stepmother. He proverbially begged forgiveness for her from her father.

17 In fact, it is Li, the first-born son of Confucius, who takes the public name of Boyu. He died at the age of fifty, while his father was still alive.

18 It is the public name of Ziqin, another of Confucius' disciples.

19 Zhong You, Zay Yu, Zilu or Jilu as a public name (542–480 B.C.), again another disciple of Confucius who achieved notable social status. He was noted for his courage and sense of justice, which did not prevent warnings from the master to proceed with more caution and restraint, given his inclination to behave impulsively. A native of Bian, within the same state of Lu, he came from a rural background. A military man and jurist, he was killed in the state of Wei, defending his lord Kong Kui.

an example to illustrate it. Jing, an official of the Duke of Wei,[20] whom they consider an excellent bursar, a model among his peers, because he always claimed to have less than he had actually achieved, except at the end of his tenure, when he reached the peak of his career and his unquestionable success was already irremediably evident. Confucius insists on this idea on several occasions, for which he exhorts us to avoid charlatanism and stubbornness, both of which are inconvenient, impolite and, therefore, not to be recommended (XIV, XXIV: 131). Especially, lack of modesty and unnecessary verbal ostentation are far removed from the facts of everyday life (XIV, XXI: 129). As will be seen in greater detail, this is one of the great concerns of the Analects, to emphasise what is manifested by what is done, the declarations of intentions with the concrete works that are carried out in daily life.

The restraint of Confucian verbal politeness can reach in its most acute version even to silence. To begin with, because Confucius is convinced that profound messages can circulate without words, as nature itself does with the four seasons of the year (XVII, XIX: 152). There is an evident semiotic awareness and a confidence that what is central to the process of transmitting messages is that they reach their destination, fulfil their purpose and communicate, regardless of the channel used to do so. If words are not necessary, there is no problem in dispensing with them, when communication comes, by the mere passage of time.

Especially men in the highest strata of society should set an example of such extreme verbal restraint. Gongming Jia relates, at the behest of Confucius, how the master Gongshu Wenzi[21] only spoke when it was time to do so, thus ensuring that his words were not unbearable (XIV, XIV: 127).

20 Wei was one of the most prominent lands during the period of the Warring Kingdoms, when it reached its peak between 445 and 370 B.C. Its royal house began in the so-called Spring and Autumn Period, from 722 B.C. onwards, settling in what are now the areas of Henan, Hebei, Shanxi and Shandong. But, as mentioned above, it was in the later period that it made its greatest impact, especially after Duke Hui proclaimed its independence as a kingdom in 344 B.C. Despite fairly productive economic reforms and some military success during this period, the death of Hui in 319 B.C. led to the decline of the Hui kingdom. Thus, when Confucius turns to the example of the bursar of the kingdom of Wei, he is appealing to what was at that time a hegemonic, or tendentially hegemonic, and therefore prestigious, reference.

21 Gongshu Wenzi seems to have been the posthumous title given to Gongsun Ba (or also Gongsun Zhi), a minister in Wei, known for his high degree of dignity, whom Confucius apparently came to know personally. He must have been an exemplary

In essence, silence was a cautious way of protecting from the world and its dangerous deviations. To persevere in the direction of benevolence could imply a refusal to listen to anything that went against good manners. In the same way it could imply the renunciation of speaking when it implied behaving incorrectly (XII, I: 112). This is, in essence, an extreme version of the cautious distance that he always advises about what comes from the outside world. Such distrust can even lead to disregarding that reality external to the individual, which also has its corresponding counterpart in the avoidance of pronouncing on it.

At other times, the renunciation of verbal activity concentrates on concrete aspects, with a high symbolic value, but at the same time as a civic strategy. The Noble Man abstains from any kind of dispute from maturity onwards (XVI, VII: 145). Doing so is a sign of the knowledge he has acquired over time, thanks to which he is able to apply maximum prudence. A prudence which also means adopting a stance as radical as the renunciation of even participating in any debate. Confucius considers unproductive such situations, both from a personal point of view and from the point of view of social harmony. Disputes do not contribute anything remarkable to the Noble Man in his formative path and ethical growth, besides not being conducive to a suitable social climate. Those who are endowed with unique knowledge are also capable of obtaining and transmitting information in a sometimes very subtle way. The teacher does not need to ask questions directly. He can infer them just by observing the behaviour of others, whether temperate, kind, courteous, moderate or simply complacent (I, X: 53). In any case, this does not mean that he renounces knowledge through verbal interaction, always among other elements of judgement. It is not in vain that he recognises that to evaluate a person it is necessary to listen to his words and know his actions (V, IX: 73).

Silence was also subject to ritual regulation in very specific circumstances. Sovereigns were silent during the three official years of mourning, corresponding to the loss of their predecessors on the throne (XIV, XLII: 133). Citizens like Confucius should observe it when eating or when in bed (X, VIII: 103).

person of recognised stature, so much that in the *Analects* he is referred to as an ethically prestigious authority.

3.4 Verbal Politeness as an Ethical Foundation

The elements discussed so far are indispensable components for a social behaviour, based on a politeness that occupies a central place in the Confucian civic project. So much so that politeness in verbal dealings with others is one of the main catalysts of benevolence, in its meaning of the term, thanks to which embarrassing situations, such as insulting others, can be avoided. Alongside it, generosity, sincerity, diligence and kindness are the instruments that generate the benevolence to which exemplary citizens aspire (XVII, VI: 149).

Sometimes, politeness does not correspond to the most widespread social habits. Confucius refers that he was criticised for entering the Great Temple asking questions, when doing so, in fact, meant observing the rule of politeness established for that occasion (III, XV: 62). Even those in charge of the Great Temple, who could be presumed to have a thorough and complete knowledge of rites and public courtesy, did not remember this rule. Confucius, on the other hand, did remember the rule, as a person who had decided to walk the path of the Noble Man.

Verbal politeness also denotes and maintains the moral order to which one aspires. In the face of a man of knowledge, three major mistakes in verbal behaviour can be made: speaking when we should not (which would be exaltation); not speaking when we should (concealment, in this case); speaking without looking at the attitude of the interlocutor's face (finally, blindness, XVI, VI: 145).

Of course, the non-verbal component accompanies, in a suitably regulated and ritualised way, the linguistically polite uses and customs. The Analects recall that Confucius himself always bowed twice when sending greetings to people of other states (X, XI: 104).

It is not always easy to exercise verbal politeness in this way. It often involves maintaining subtle balances, carefully weighing linguistic choices so as not to go too far in one direction or the other. The greatest difficulties in this respect are in dealing with servants and women. Confucius refuses to be detached from them, given the obvious disenchantment and tension that this would entail. But, at the same time, he warns that granting them trust may lead to a relationship that is too bold, which he considers inappropriate (XVII, XXV: 154).

In addition, individuals should always orient themselves according to their place in the social hierarchy in which they operate. When addressing people of lower rank, it is appropriate to use an accommodating gesture. On the other hand, with those of higher rank it is advisable to maintain a more natural countenance. With the prince, people can only act with utmost respect (X, II: 101).

Such extreme and concentrated respect, at times almost sacred, can even lead to words not wanting to come out, to the most sumptuous silence, such as that which must be observed in front of the throne (X, IV: 102).

In any of these circumstances, offences must be avoided, especially towards superiors. Such actions are typical of people who want to cause confusion, insofar as they contravene filial love, always in the Confucian meaning of that concept. For Lu's master, it is the real driving force of life, both in the public and private spheres. Filial piety governs domestic relations within the household, while brotherly love does the same in social life (I, II: 51). This is such a central idea that Confucius underlines it by putting it in the mouth of You Ruo, one of the master's most devoted disciples, who is said to be one of the compilers of the Analects, or at least one of the authors of part of them.[22]

Politeness concretely affects the communicative relationship with the Noble Men, also with its requirements and demands, sometimes implicit, sometimes bordering on the overtly formal. To begin with, no communication with such a person can be approached without a solid education. Confucius refers to the ubiquitous Odes, without a thorough and profound knowledge of which no such interaction is conceivable (XVI, XIII: 146). On this point, he certainly maintains a firm and unambiguous position, since he expresses his conviction that superior things can only be explained to those who are above mediocrity (VI, XIX: 80). Below it, the only thing he can find is incomprehension of the depths of his approaches and incorrectness. Here he is again very explicit. People who are incapable of talking about justice—one of the pillars of his ethics—but only about little things, are completely removed from the possibility of finding correctness (XV, XVIII: 138).

In any case, this rigour should not be interpreted in such hermetic terms as to prevent any form of intercommunication between people who are distant in their training. In another passage (VIII, X: 91) he recommends that the exemplary man should ask and take an interest in those who are not as skilled as he is, that he should talk to those endowed with few qualities and that he should always avoid any form of dispute, even when he is offended. One of the functions of

---

22 You Ruo (518 B.C.–457 B.C.), also a native of Lu, was one of the master's closest disciples during his lifetime. Famous for his excellent memory and love of antiquity, he initially seemed destined to be the recipient of Confucius' legacy after his death. However, he lost the confidence of his fellow disciples, so he ended up founding his own school. Within this school it seems that the first sections of the *Analects* may have been written. On other occasions he also used the names Zi Ruo or Youzi.

leaders is precisely to evaluate the words of others and to exercise their administrative action. Those who are endowed with this responsibility must avoid administrative promotion because of the words that someone may have said, just as they must always take them into consideration, regardless of who the author may be (XV, XXII: 13). Therefore, there is an exercise of necessary weighting, of assessment without pre-established criteria that can condition decisions on the matters being managed. In the background of this consideration lies another of the constants of Confucian thought. Words are not the only clue to judge a person's moral condition. It is necessary to check whether his words correspond to his actions, whether there is congruence between what is said and what is done.

3.5 Exemplarity and Correctness in Leading Groups

Kings themselves are not exempt from strictly adhering to the precepts of courtly linguistic rules. In reply to a question from the Duke of Ting,[23] Confucius does not hesitate to point out that the sovereign should address his ministers courteously, even command them in this way (III, XIX: 63). However, the verbal leeway to which all, rulers and subjects alike, must conform will ultimately depend on the very social and political dynamics that rulers have been able to set in motion within their societies. In well-ruled states, it is possible to speak and act boldly. On the other hand, in poorly governed states, it will be more advisable to speak out cautiously (XIV, IV: 125).

The performance of the administration of society, concretely between the sovereign and his high dignitaries, is equally subject to utmost care in verbal performance. Everything that surrounds the ruler, what he does and what he says, what he manifests and what he dictates, is the mirror in which the citizens look. Therefore, it is a model as well, on whose exemplarity the success of

---

23 Duke Ting was one of Confucius' greatest political supporters. When he was fifty-two years old, he entrusted him with the administration of the central Lu region. Confucius' performance became legendary, attributing to him absolute social peace in practically all spheres. He also promoted and extended education, as well as increasing protection for the neediest, the elderly and children. That was the beginning of a successful administrative path for a while, in which he went on to take care of public works and justice for the whole state. Something must have gone wrong at some point, because it is said that Confucius left the Lu administration disappointed by the Duke of Ting's lack of continuity in his moral principles.

a society depends to a large extent. This is an idea that is constantly repeated in the Analects. The only way to demand correct behaviour from citizens is through the exemplary exercise of government. Thus, communication events in this area should not be left to chance, outside the framework of ethical precepts that are ultimately proposed in the Analects.

Therefore, for Confucius, it is of utmost importance to pay close attention to the communication that takes place within the exercise of government, both on the part of its leaders, its officials and its users.

The rulers have their own verbal patterns that must be followed regularly. Nor is it the case that, from a general perspective, the type of language has a determining role to play in the first place. In reality, there is no single phrase that can be beneficial, or detrimental to the government of a kingdom. But proverbs do summarise that thought and are highly recommendable (XIII, XV: 121). In more specific matters, verbal guidelines are somewhat more restrictive. Among the factors that can encourage the cultivation of benevolence, orders to inferiors should be given as if a sacrifice was going to be celebrated, as well as to avoid murmuring against oneself, one's family and one's country (XII, II: 112). On the other hand, to obtain and hold public office, he considers it necessary to have a proven ability to listen to many things, to separate the dubious from the doubtful and to speak only of what is known to avoid being criticised, another of Confucius' constant concerns (II, VIII: 58). Likewise, to keep away from complaints and gossip, rulers should intensify a precept common to all citizens, by being very demanding of themselves and declining the least amount of responsibility for others (XV, XIV: 137). If slander is pernicious as a matter of principle, the managers of social life must take special care to banish it from their surroundings and from their persons.

To continue, such intense diligence must be employed in the actions of the rulers that Confucius proposes to formalize the protocol of these linguistic interventions as much as possible, even establishing a specific figure in the court, a specialist solely in charge of speaking and dealing with ambassadors and visitors, such as Chi (V, VII: 72).

For this reason, the official writing should be conducted with utmost care and extreme precision in its production. Thus, as an example to draw inspiration from, he refers to the profuse elaboration of the sovereign's decrees, an irrefutable example of teamwork, with clearly established and specialised tasks: Pi Chen was responsible for preparing the first draft, whose content would be revised by

Shishu, while the stylistic correction was the responsibility of Ziyu before Zichan gave the final touch and concluded with an elegant form (XIV, IX: 126).[24]

The development of communication within the court is not less ritualised. The names of the highest exponents of state are formally regulated, concretely that of the sovereign's wife. Her husband will refer to her as "consort", while she will call herself "princess". For the citizens of the country, her subjects, she will be the "consort of the sovereign", while foreigners will be able to choose between "little sovereign" and "consort of the sovereign" (XVI, XIV: 147). Such a complex distribution of terminology refers to two very relevant issues in the Confucian view. On the one hand, the asymmetry between men and women, quite evident in many passages of the Analects, reaches even to the highest levels of the social pyramid. There is no such heterogeneous nomenclature for the prince, who is always in all circumstances and before any interlocutor. On the other hand, the firmness of civic values is such that it knows no exceptions, taking precedence over any other consideration or circumstance, as is the case with the absolute and non-negotiable benchmark of social life. Moreover, the sovereign cannot just call herself by any name but must do so in accordance with rules that bind her, in a very constrained manner. Not even the throne can avoid these values. On the contrary, given its position of absolute hegemony within society, it has to observe them all the more scrupulously, insofar as they are the benchmark by which the rest of the components of the social body of the state it rules must be guided. As can be seen, this is a recurrent idea that appears and returns repeatedly in many passages of the Analects.

The exercise of high responsibilities within the administration of states leaves an imprint for the rest of an individual's life. A social, but also an ethical, status is attained which remains forever. It has corresponding linguistic consequences. After someone has occupied a high civil servant's position, he could never keep quiet about what he had to say (XIV, XXIII: 12). What was once an administrative obligation has been transferred to ethical routines.

24 Confucius is referring to the Duchy of Zheng. Pi Chen was a leading figure in it, highly skilled in matters of strategy. Shishu was concerned with aesthetic matters, Ziyu studied the neighbouring states, and Zichan was at the apex of this political and administrative organization as its prime minister.

3.6 Fame Caution

The leaders of society are mirrors in which the rest of the society looks. That is why they enjoy a prestige that is as evident as it is inevitable. This popularity, this fame, is of considerable concern to Lu's master. It is not in vain that he devotes several reflections to this question and how it manifests itself using language.

In this respect, his attitude is only partially ambiguous. It is true that, in principle, fame is not at all among the concerns of exemplary men. On the contrary, they even disdain it to a certain extent. Ethically elevated beings, human exemplars in every respect, do not suffer when they are unknown (XV, VIII: 138). Among other reasons, their kingdom is not of this world or, at the least, straddles two worlds. These beings prefer Heaven to know their goodness, rather than worldly fame (XIV, XXVII: 131). Moreover, fame seems to be a part of the fickleness of the world that is so easily accommodated in the rhetoric that it so repudiates. It is a consequence to be avoided of the inordinate weighting of others. Words should never be promoted which might lead to the unwarranted promotion of anyone. Extreme care must be taken in what is said, since one can be reputed and achieve fame by a word alone. And the opposite is also possible with the same verbal economy: one word is enough to sink a person's prestige and remove him from social respect (XIX, XXV: 164). However, on other occasions he is somewhat more indulgent. On the one hand, it is undeniable that the fame exists so strongly that it sometimes exceeds even what can be conveyed by writings, or what can be made known by sages, as is the case with the rites of the Xia dynasty (III, IX: 61).

On the other hand, fame, at least in some of its meanings, is also an exponent of a person's most profound virtues contemplated by this ethic. Thus, Min Ziquian[25] was a repository of true filial piety, because everyone spoke of him in the same way as his parents and brothers did (XI, IV: 106).

It is true that fame can even transcend the very consistency of language. Incidentally, the Analects recall that Yao's magnificence was such that his subjects were unable to name him (VIII, XIX: 93).

In other passages Confucius' indulgence even leads to doubt where he really stands on the matter. At times he seems not only indulgent but actually prone

---

25 One of Confucius' (536 B.C.–487 B.C.) most beloved disciples, also a native of Lu. Outside the court he was known as Min Sun. He is one of the twenty-four models of Confucian filial piety.

to fame when he states that Noble Men dislike the fact that their name is not remembered after their death, that they do not maintain an enduring fame after the passage of time (XV, XIX: 138). He even goes so far as to establish a chronological limit in biography, after which it becomes worrying not to have achieved the appropriate notoriety. He reminds us that it is important to be known around the age of forty or fifty. Otherwise, when these people are not heard of, they run the risk of being considered and treated without respect, one of the pillars of Confucian life (IX, XXII: 99).

At times it even seems an obligation to contribute to the spread of that fame, always from the strict approach and judgement that wisdom gives. So, he recommends praising, even with emphasis, those who really deserve it (XV, XXIV: 139), as well as speaking and spreading the excellences of other men, an act that he even considers satisfactory (XVI, V: 145). Moreover, contributing to the social dissemination of honour—which means remembering the name and figure of exemplary persons—is one of the obligations of those who enjoy the privileged formation of a society. From it, it is necessary to pity the incapacity of others, to praise the goodness of those who possess it and to honour with all possible merits those who are considered illustrious (XIX, III: 159).

Probably, the solution to this apparent contradiction is to be found in Yan Yuan's book (XXII, XX: 116), when he draws a very subtle, but extraordinarily sharp and relevant distinction between a famous man and a well-known man. Famous is the one who examines the words, observes their expressions and is humble. On the other hand, the well-known man pretends to be as just mentioned, but is incapable of carrying it out. There is a clearly ethical background to this distinction, which makes fame correspond, roughly speaking, with the Noble Man and the status of the well known with other characters in social life who have not attained this degree of depth, knowledge and ethical perfection. It is more than likely that this concept of fame corresponded little to the social reality among his contemporaries. Only Confucius is not positing an analysis of causes, circumstances and interests in terms of whether someone is a repository of social and worldly fame or not. His model is an ideal model, a proposal from his ethical perspective, showing an enormous awareness of the decisive role played by symbols, by famous individuals, in the imaginary of a society. Therefore, it becomes fundamental in the transmission of its principles and fundamental patterns of life.

3.7 Verbal Exponents of Inner Ethics

In addition to precepts, rules of politeness, guidelines for the different social strata or advice for the correct administration of fame, the Analects also contain an intense guide of verbal behaviour that denote the inner transformation that their ethics presupposes, while, at the same time, contributing in no small measure to exercising it.

This inner sphere of communication in Confucian ethics naturally stems from the very choice of language used by individuals. Not just any kind of words are acceptable, just as not just any kind of actions are acceptable. Confucius thinks in terms of irreproachable exemplarity. It is loyal and sincere words that are to be used by those who seek personal perfection and, with it, the betterment of their society. Nor are isolated, out-of-tune words or actions worthless. On the contrary, he considers that this verbal action dominated by sincerity must be matched by honourable deeds in order to achieve the right way of acting (XV, V: 136). This is another of the central issues in the Analects in relation to communication, to which the text returns on different occasions, with innumerable nuances. At times, these needs for maximum congruence between words and actions justify the greatest possible verbal economy. Confucius once again appeals to the ancients to remind us that actions must match words. For this very reason, those longed-for and mystified exemplars seem to have been reluctant to speak. Thus, we must try to prevent words from failing to live up to the commendations of their deeds (IV, XXII: 69). This is the path of the Noble Man who puts his words into practice before he speaks them, and then speaks in accordance with his actions (II, XIII: 57). Therefore, these beings who have attained the highest degree of knowledge and inner perfection can afford to be slow of speech and diligent of action (IV, XXIV: 70). It is true that this ability to take advantage of the positive things that come from outside, in practising what one hears, should follow rhythms appropriate to each person. Sometimes it is convenient that it is conducted with pause and prudence, for those who are fast and accelerated. For those who are at the opposite extreme, their pause recommends greater celerity in putting into practice the knowledge received (XI, XXI: 110).

Such congruence links to what is said, but no less it does to what is heard. There is no point in hearing things that are supposed to be good and not putting them into practice. This seemed to happen to Zigong, who was not inclined to take advantage of the examples that life was giving him (V, XIII: 73). On the other hand, the Analects recommend assenting to the words of warning, as a first step, almost as an immediate reaction, awaiting the truly substantial, which consists in understanding in depth the content of what they warn. Certainly, it is even possible to experience satisfaction in the face of good and friendly advice. But what is truly fundamental consists in being able to put it into practice and develop it (IX, XXIII: 99).

Wise words are of essential importance and an indispensable basis for learning about the Higher-Self. So much so that they have an intrinsic value that allows them to be detached from any other kind of conditioning or circumstance. The Analects suggest that Confucius had heard the discourses of those who seek the Way, even though he has never seen them (XVI, XI: 146). Then, the substance is in the words and in listening to them, because they are enough to receive convenient and profitable teachings.

The correspondence between words and actions does not seem to be a negligible or unimportant matter in the eyes of Confucius. On the contrary, its noncompliance, in principle, has serious consequences. When this congruence does not occur, does not form part of a Noble Man's daily routine, he loses his status as a Noble Man. This is precisely what happened to Ji Zicheng[26] (XII, VIII: 114).

Only, it should be considered that such an apparently firm symbiosis could be nuanced under certain circumstances that may justify it. Both words and actions had to be accommodated to the inheritance inherent in the ethical principles being preached, even to the point of attenuating such intense solidarity. Hui of Liuxia[27] and Shaolian surrendered their will, even humiliated their persons, but their words accorded with reason and their actions with reflection. Yuzhong and Yiyi,[28] though they lived hidden and away from men, though they used careless words, yet they kept their bodies pure and their carelessness was only attributed to circumstances. Thus, their honour is safe (XVIII, VIII: 157).

What is not inadmissible is the lack of commitment, of effective linkage, to the society to which Confucius and his disciples commit themselves to

---

26 Minister of Wei, the state of the Warring Kingdoms period, from V to 221 B.C. It comprised the states of Quin and Qi, corresponding to the present-day areas of Henan, Hebei, Shanxi and Shandong.

27 Zhan Huo (720–621 B.C.) changed his court name to Qin in his fifties. He was a pre-eminent politician, who ruled the Liuxia district within the kingdom of Lu. He was considered a man of great virtue and a moral example to his contemporaries.

28 Confucius turns to several political figures, well known and in positions of responsibility at the time, but who, like Hui of Liuxia, were esteemed for their high moral rectitude. Thus, they personify the Confucian ideal of the ruler as a mirror of virtue from which his subjects should draw inspiration.

collaborate effectively and efficiently. This is one of the great arguments against Taoist approaches. Jieyu, who embodies the quintessential Taoist sage, is portrayed as a madman (VIII, V: 156). Confucius, at first, tries to address him. Eventually Jieyu escapes and flees, symbolising his lack of engagement with the world and time, with the society in which he lives.

References

Krammer, S. N. (1968). The Babel of Tongues. A Sumerian version. *Journal of the American Oriental Society*, *88*(1), 108-111.

Liverani, M. (2008). *El antiguo Oriente: historia, sociedad y economía*. Barcelona: Crítica.

Maturana, H., & Varela, F. (1984). *El árbol del conocimiento*. Madrid: Lumen.

4

Verbal Behavioural Patterns

This conception of communication that Confucius' thought conveys through the Analects is synthesized in a couple of principles. The strict observance of these principles leads to exemplary behaviour, not only linguistically but also socially and humanly. These three dimensions—the species, the individuals and the societies they form—are inextricably linked in Confucian ethics as a whole. Therefore, communication and language merely reflect a larger conception of life.

In any case, it should be emphasised that these principles neither exist nor operate in a fractioned way. The observance of only some of them does not result in proper verbal behaviour, nor in the manifestation of a correct social and ethical position. Again, as in the rest of his system, proper communication is put in truly strict terms, but at the same time with extraordinary coherence. It is necessary to observe all the principles I will try to deal with below. The Noble Man does not neglect a single one of them. There is no possibility of partial indulgence or of hierarchical gradation between one principle and another. All of them are indispensable and must be put into practice, which is not without an intrinsic logic; Confucius does not think of any of these elements by mere chance. Everything in his doctrine is valuable or, at least, he incorporates it from the awareness of considering it so. Therefore, it would have made no sense to be lukewarm about any of his principles, in communicative or any other matter. After all, what he is proposing in the Analects is nothing less than an intense and solid ethics.

4.1 Rectitude

From the congruence between words and actions follows a linguistic behaviour based on rectitude, a vehicle for both encouraging and cementing it. When fair agreements have been made between honourable people, the word given must be kept unswervingly, as Youzi once did (I, XIII: 53). Such grave, upright and consistent language is one of the identifying characteristics of the Noble Man (XIX, IX: 160). Moreover, verbal rectitude is an extension of civic rectitude and, ultimately, of the personal rectitude by which a man must conduct himself in all aspects of his life.

This general principle, respect, must be especially careful when dealing with the past, the ultimate benchmark on which Confucius formally draws his inspiration, as has been amply demonstrated on so many other occasions. He does not allow any concessions to respect, to the point of recommending that it is preferable not even to speak of matters that have already passed, let alone to protest about them or accuse any of their protagonists of anything (III, XII: 63).

Of course, rectitude has direct consequences for behaviour in general so that it serves as a focal point for other ethical principles. The Noble and Upright Man is also impartial. He preserves the truth without doubt or hesitation. Therefore, he acts consistently in a sincere manner, while logically avoiding anything casts doubt on the firm and unambiguous choice he has made. Like life in all senses, communication reflects these values and must be guided by them.

4.2 Equanimity

Rather than shying away from disputes, the Noble Man avoids taking sides in them, at least formally (VII, XX: 88). Confucius thinks that language is too valuable to be wasted on matters that hinder the proper flow of the Way (of moral and ethical improvement, of course). Moreover, this reflection occurs in the context of a very singular episode in the Analects. Confucius considers that Duke Zhao has an adequate knowledge of the rites. However, when the Minister of Justice Chen[29] notices that the nobleman has made a mistake, he doubts that

29 Zhao (or Chao, in other transcriptions) was one of the most prominent states during

a Noble Man, like Confucius was, is always impartial. At this point Confucius introduces this recommendation, with an evident hint of distance. Such a stance contrasts with his unequivocal commitment to reality, to society and to life. Therefore, he is deploying the guiding principles of a profuse ethics which do involve a considerably explicit taking of sides, which only Noble Men are capable of crowning. The passage is also surprising because it is precisely about rites. It is true that on other occasions he warns of the little profit to be gained from meddling in worldly affairs, from which it is best for people of high moral education to distance themselves. However, he does attach crucial importance to rites. Moreover, he insists on numerous occasions on the desirability of rulers being particularly scrupulous in this respect, because of the exemplary effect it has on the population. So, like Minister Chen, the reader of the Analects at this point would probably expect censure, to whatever degree, of Duke Zhao. This is not the case, to everyone's bewilderment. It is not because it was most probably not the intention of Lu's master at the time to address the question of rites or the obligation of nobles to follow the precepts of the higher status like any other individual. What he is trying to emphasise is the inappropriateness of engaging in discussions between private individuals, even when they are of such high rank as a duke and a minister of justice, even when they concern such fundamental aspects as rites for the smooth running and good governance of society. It would seem to take the primordial and non-negotiable nature of rites for granted so that discussing them may be manifestly idle.

Equanimity is a formalisation of the intrinsic nature of individuals, not least their ability to communicate through language. Confucius reminds us that the wise and the foolish are the only ones who do not get upset (XVII, III: 149), those who are capable of using language that flows through balanced, equidistant channels, far from excessive passions.

But, in addition to not wanting to use language in vain, Confucius is seriously wary of making it an absolute parameter of truth. He knows that it is subject to numerous influences, conditioning and dangers. That is why he warns of the convenience of using it with caution and advises to administer it with precaution, at all levels of life, from the most modest to the highest levels. Thus, in order to obtain public office, he advises to listen to many things, to separate the

the Warring Kingdoms. Located between today's Inner Mongolia, Hebei, Shanxi and Shaanxi provinces, it had to survive its continuous border problems between the powerful Qi and Wei.

doubtful ones and to speak only of what it is known to avoid being criticised (II, XVIII: 58). Incidentally, he reminds us that there is not a single sentence that can be beneficial, or detrimental, to the government of a kingdom. He only grants this power to the proverbs, as has already been pointed out, from the conviction that they are capable of condensing a wise and profound thought (XIII, XV: 121). It is not in vain that proverbs are an inheritance from that past which he reveres.

Verbal equanimity also manifests itself through behaviour that is adaptive to communication situations and interlocutors. Confucius himself is an example of this, when in his village he behaved with simplicity, as if he were incapable of speaking. On the other hand, he spoke a lot on court, but always with care (X, I: 101). Each context, each type of interaction, required its own verbal patterns, inherent to the variation of the environment. Linguistic virtue is manifested in the ability to adapt in an effective and pertinent manner to the demands of each specific case, in full harmony with what sociolinguistics has nowadays called functional repertoire. That is the adaptation of the use of language to each specific communication situation.

4.3 Sincerity

Sincerity is another extension of the principle of righteousness that must govern the actions of exemplary citizens, also in their verbal behaviour, as a further part of their life's actions. Sincere words are indispensable in their friendly relations, as an unmistakable sign of an upright man. This is a behaviour to be maintained along with the esteem of the illustrious or the service to their fathers and the king. It goes without saying that Noble Men carry it to its highest expression and have it incorporated among their distinguishing features (XVI, X: 146). It is such an essential trait for good coexistence that they must contemplate it even in untrained people (I, VII: 52). Moreover, acting in this way is still a way of embracing what is purely intrinsic to the human condition. Insincerity seems to him to be against nature, as if a small cart were unrigged (III, XXII: 59). But the truth is that sincerity supports any linguistic performance. Also, those that can be more compromising, such as warnings to friends, must be pronounced with loyalty and sincerity (XII, XIII: 117).

Of course, it is considered a virtue proper to Noble Men. Among the traits that characterise them are their movements and attitudes far from violence and carelessness, gestures always corrected in accordance with the canons, and words and exclamations that are free from coarseness and vulgarity—all of which are regulated by sincerity (VIII, IV: 91). Thus, these privileged men are characterised by using words that are solid and sincere (XI, XX: 109). They are also cautious in foreseeing the lie and turning away from it (XIV, XXIII: 131). Before they die, their words attain the highest excellence (VIII, IV: 91), which is a recognition of the value accumulated by experience.

Such is the importance of this trait that it is also obligatory for rulers. This is one of the virtues that the people will imitate from the ruler if he is able to behave in this way (XIII, IV: 119), a virtue that is complemented by justice and respect for rites. Zhou, among other things, won over the masses by his sincerity (XX, I: 165).

4.4 Names

So far, the precepts governing Confucian communication have been connected to a greater or lesser extent with the principle of righteousness, which has acted as the backbone of all of them. Unlike it, in the case of names there is no direct link with the principle of righteousness, although it does not completely lose reference to it. In any case, names cover a wide spectrum of aspects of social interaction.

The Analects do not avoid one of the major issues present in all Chinese thought of the Pre-Qin period. For Lao-Tse, one of the greatest limitations of human nature lay in names. Since all things exist because of a first principle, the Dao, and the Dao is unfathomable by its very nature, names only give a semblance of what things really are. Hence, names only generate distrust, because of the suspicion that they ultimately mislead humans.

The problem of the correctness of names is also present in the Analects, though in a sense ostensibly different from the one just discussed. Confucius' concern with the correctness of names is directly linked to the organisation of social life, not to any philosophical speculation. So much so that, in his opinion, the first duty of a sovereign is precisely to see to the correctness of names and, if necessary, to rectify them (XIII, III: 118).

But when are names considered incorrect? Such dissonance, of extreme gravity, arises when words do not conform to what they represent. If that happens, the affairs of the state are not properly and efficiently settled. Then, neither rites nor music will be performed correctly, nor will there be justice in punishments. Names can also reflect the positive qualities of people, with the consequent exemplary character that this entails for the other members of the community.

Gongwenzi is given the syllable "wen" because he is an active person and was not ashamed to question his inferiors (V, XIV: 73).

Therefore, the Noble Man requires that names correspond to facts, to avoid any improper source that disturbs his path and his mission in the construction of a better society (XIII, III: 118). Or, in other words, names are required to correspond to their meaning (XV, XLIII: 143). It is not for nothing that he considers a person to be exemplary when he strives to ensure that his words are believed by others and his actions correspond to them (XIII, XX: 122).

The correctness of names, in this sense that Confucius attributes to it, is a skill that is acquired through training and then exercised through ethically exemplary daily action. Therefore, those who have knowledge, those who have attained that higher degree of deepening, do not err, neither with men nor with words (XV, VII: 136).

"He who does not know the meaning of words cannot know men." This is not just any fragment, but the last reflection with which the Analects conclude (XX, III: 166).

4.5 Harmful Linguistic Behaviours

The communicative precepts of the Confucian ideal have their obverse side. Their list of ways of using language, that sometimes led away from virtue, sometimes show that a person is far from the Way and persists in this error. These harmful elements are also the foreseeable by-product of language misuse, which he warns about with some regularity in the Analects.

An old nuisance that appears with relative regularity in these pages, rhetoric, is at the top of this list in the negative sector of communication. It has already been mentioned that Confucius shows a real aversion to rhetoric, to hollow eloquence, although he approaches it with commendable consideration. Such is the detachment he shows to it that he recommends to the Noble Man not to promote anyone by the words he speaks. Nor does he admit of taking into consideration the words spoken, irrespective of who their author may be. (XV, XXII: 139).

In any case, the rejection of rhetoric disallows any other verbal behaviour indiscriminately. Nor is it enough to guard against empty words. It is not in vain that he reminds us that to speak carelessly is to throw away virtue (XVII, XIV: 151). An individual must therefore be aware of what he speaks and how he speaks.

This is another of the countless episodes in which Confucius applies the golden mean to the most mundane and trivial aspects of daily life, always in pursuit of a balanced equilibrium. The use of language must also follow this balanced path: neither abuse its pomposity nor lack decorum and communicability.

This attitude is particularly evident when it comes to eloquence. It is true that there have been notable figures, such as Zai Yu[30] and Zigong, characterised by their brilliant use of words. This is certainly a form of distinction and should be recognised as such. Just as others are noted for their political skill, depth of study or virtue, so eloquent usage is a personal characteristic to be admired by their fellow citizens (XI, II: 106). The position of the Analects is indeed relevant to the Confucian approach in this regard. Rhetorical excellence is worthy of social admiration, but it is listed alongside other social excellences worthy of appreciation, such as virtue. In essence, we are returning to the original approach to verbal pomposity. It is another plane different from virtue which does not deny social appreciation and consideration. In any case, it is not part of the instruments necessary to follow the virtuous path, ethical exemplarity, which is the ultimate aim of the work. In any case, indulgence in eloquent behaviour has its limits. When it is an exponent of mastery of language, we have just seen that it grants them a certain margin of acceptance. However, it manifests itself much more radically in relation to verbal excesses, over which it extends a critical rule, uniform and without exception, which also includes people of prestige, such as the ritualist Two (VI, XIV: 79).

On the other hand, language should never be a vehicle for circumventing social hierarchy. Offence to superiors is at odds with filial piety and brotherly love, virtues that are more than cardinal in the ethical scheme defended by Confucianism. It is none other than Ziyou, who is responsible for expressing himself with such rotundity (I, II: 51) in this respect. In the same paragraph, the beloved disciple of the master Confucius, with such a continuous presence and prominence in the Analects, insists on the idea that offences against superiors are typical of people who delight in producing confusion. That is no more than altering the established order of society which is also a map according to which the individual is oriented, organised and located.

30 Also, Zai Wo on other occasions.

4.6 Attention to Writing

Almost all the communicative concerns of the Analects concentrate on orality. This is very revealing of the structure of the transmission of knowledge in Chinese society at the time, but also all of Confucius' acute awareness.

In fact, Confucius stresses orality, which is the vast domain of linguistic interactions in his time. Writing was reserved for a literate minority, which was quite exceptional in an ungrammatical society. It is true that the knowledge required to attain the status of a Noble Man comes in part from the written channel, which therefore becomes a necessary condition for acquiring it. The Analects repeatedly appeal to the argument of the formative and ethical authority of the Odes. No one who is not literate, who is not sufficiently proficient in writing to read and interpret them, will be in a position to begin their formative journey. It is just that this is a reality that is implicit, taken for granted and assumed as such in these terms. Moreover, training is not exhausted in writing, nor does it cease to be subject to highly formalised social guidelines. The Analects themselves are reliable and direct testimony of an oral teaching, which is exercised by transmitting thoughts—sentences on many occasions—in direct interactions with his disciples, as the work reflects that Confucius himself did. On the other hand, writing, as the great formal instrument of administration, had its own clearly established guidelines and procedures. Therefore, it did not constitute a matter that could be clarified or specified.

In fact, the Analects do not suggest any kind of duality, let alone opposition, between the spoken and written uses of languages, or between the possible functions of one or the other. However, there is a curious passage in which a traveller engraves a message from Confucius on a belt in order to keep it always in mind (XV, V: 136). Writing as a guarantor of the durability of messages and their contents has been universal throughout history and across cultures, which curiously reappears in a work such as the Analects, a profound reflection on human beings and their behaviour in society.

4.7 Instruction

To achieve not only these communicative abilities but also this high moral status, it is necessary to undergo training, in which words logically play a more significant role. A relatively high level of training is necessary to enter the profound messages, those of the path that leads to the ultimate wisdom. Confucius' words can be heard, or read, but not those that refer to the nature of man or the way ordained by Heaven. The foundations, the conceptual supports of his proposal, require another way of access (V, XIII: 73). These chasms of knowledge can only be reached through introspection and the capacities that each person has been able to learn and develop.

This approach is a manifestation of the open spirit of his thought, albeit sifted by a crude realism that is at the same time necessary. His ethics are unrestricted from the outset and are predicated for any human being. However, while developing it, very few people have the capacity to enter the ultimate interstices of knowledge, of human nature, and its relationship with the cosmos and with life.

When a person is in the situation and conditions to enter this training, Confucius recommends proceeding with order and method (IX, X: 97). To begin with, one should take the right points of reference. The Noble Man fears the words of the wise (XVI, VIII: 145), which is to be translated as taking them as an uncontroversial reference, from which to confront his own existence. Hence, he avoids not behaving according to these examples. To continue, descending to the more concrete field, he himself takes it upon himself to teach literature, conduct, fidelity and truthfulness (VII, XXIV: 87). Of course, the ancient Odes, which continue to be present in the Analects, are an indispensable source of knowledge because they are directly linked to the traditions received from earlier times. In addition to this fundamental task, they have the usefulness of allowing us to learn the names of birds, quadrupeds, plants and trees, broadening and consolidating the worldview of those who delve into them (XVII, IX: 150). Therefore, it is not surprising that they are among Confucius' favourite topics of conversation, along with history and the maintenance of rites (VII, XVIII: 56). It is relatively indifferent whether this corresponds exactly to the biographical reality of the character. I understand that what he transcribes is a scholastic focus which, to a large extent, summarises and condenses the real cardinal concerns of this ethical proposal.

In any case, the approach to these subjects is not enough to develop the necessary depth to enable us to walk the Path in an adequate manner. It is necessary to question the causes that explain the functioning of ordinary life, an aspect that constitutes the initial step to enter Wisdom (XV, XV: 138). It is an universal principle with a wide motivational spectrum: of science, of knowledge, of introspection, of philosophical reflection. But it is also a frame of mind, an attitude towards life and its circumstances, even the most everyday ones, which manifests itself continuously, even in the tiniest details. Confucius made himself aware of even the smallest details, even when he attended the temple (X, XIV: 104).

5

The Contemporary Potential of the Analects: A Complex Reading from the Perspective of the Communicative Event

The Confucian text, so rich in nuances linked to communication, admits another reading that is considerably closer, or even fully susceptible of being integrated within the assumptions of contemporary linguistics. This fact underlines something that was mentioned at the beginning of these pages, the surprising validity of Confucian thought through the centuries. So much so that the content of the Analects on communication can be "translated" or "taken up" in the light of contemporary science.

All these contributions ultimately touch on some of the components of a communicative event, as would be expected from D. Hymes' formulation of it in the early 1970s. Of course, any transmission of information by means of human language, without exception, constitutes a communicative event according to the classic proposal of Hymes and his sociolinguistic school, the ethnography of speech. This event is made up of seven components, very illustratively condensed in the very famous acronym SPEAKING. That is:

1. setting and scene,
2. participants,
3. ends,
4. acts sequence,
5. key,

6. instrumentalities,
7. standards and
8. genre.

Although each of these is clearly delimited, Hymes himself insistently warns that none of them acts alone, so they must be examined from the totality of the resulting system they form.

In the Analects all the components of the communicative event are present, to a greater or lesser degree, naturally with a different calligraphy. Moreover, in the Confucian text, they often point to that interrelated perspective that Hymes was thinking of. In some ways, if the analogy holds despite the obvious huge distance in all senses, we could say that the work is also a kind of guide to the ethically relevant communicative event. This is not to say that all the components have the same weight. This eminently ethical purpose intensifies the presence of some components more than others. To return to the numerical reference, the Analects contain the following presence of the communicative event throughout its pages (Table 5.1).

Table 5.1. The components of the communicative event in the Analects

Component	Absolute data	%
Setting and scene	29	14.7
Participants	44	22.11
Ends	7	3.51
Sequence	1	0.50
Key	25	12.56
Instruments	65	32.66
Standards	18	9.04
Gender	4	2.01
Event	6	3.01
	199	

The situation can be summarised as shown in Figure 5.1.

Components of the communicative event of the
Analects

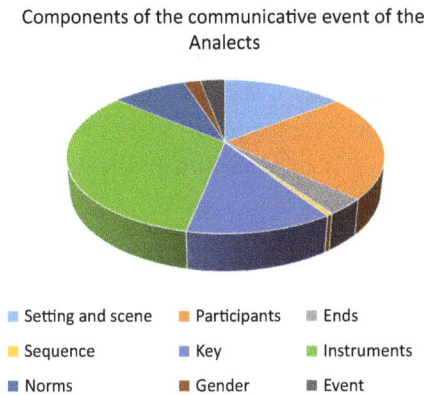

- ■ Setting and scene
- ■ Participants
- ▥ Ends
- ■ Sequence
- ■ Key
- ■ Instruments
- ■ Norms
- ■ Gender
- ■ Event

Figure 5.1. Components of the communicative event of the Analects

5.1 Setting and Scene

Arguably, Confucius is more concerned with (psychological) scenes than (physical) settings, not so much in terms of priority as in terms of operationality. Scenes are highly established in his world and therefore also in his perception of social dynamics. There are very clear and formalised procedures for behaving at court, in the presence of the sovereign or in the temple, to mention three particularly marked and socially relevant spheres. On the other hand, the scenes, entirely linked to the emotional and psychological, are more subject to the form given to them by the doctrinal body he is proposing, on which they depend entirely. Sincerity (XIII, IV: 119; II, XII: 59; XII, XXI: 157), detachment from charlatanism (XIV, XXIV: 131) or the ability not to get upset (XVI, III: 148) are other forms of the psychological disposition in which the ideal communication in which Confucius thinks must develop. Of course, this communicative disposition is a direct correlate of the profile that corresponds to the Noble Man.

Generally speaking, the *Analects* are not overly concerned with settings. Nor do they disregard them altogether, not least because they detect contextual settings that are decisive in their entirety, including their verbal language. To mention a prototypical example, when a high dignitary is in front of the monarch, he must follow a very strict and pre-established communicative pattern.

But outside such obvious and marked situations, these references are very occasional, if not sporadic.[31] It was to be expected. It has been repeatedly stated here that Confucius is interested in the background of things, their ethical content, without exceptions or extenuations. Therefore, the setting in which the communication takes place is to some extent secondary. In any of its possible versions, in any physical context, in any setting, the Noble Man must behave in a relevant and appropriate manner, in accordance with his high moral status.

The scene is distinct in its ability to transcribe the emotional or psychological component of the communicative activity, or performance of individuals in general. The scene is linked to very central questions of its ethics. Verbal language must convey credibility through the words used. They must also be the result of a state of mind committed to the acts performed by individuals, following the principle of congruence. This kind of communication can only be achieved through the sincerity of the individuals. Therefore, communication exercised in these terms shows the individuals of exceptional ethics to their peers and makes them examples for the community. But this is only possible when renouncing the evanescent fatuousness of social life, developing an exceptional capacity to distance from it and not allow it to affect or alter the Noble Man.[32]

5.2 Participants[33]

The participants in the communicative event are nuanced in the Confucian perspective. In fact, they are one of the components to which the *Analects* pay most attention. It makes sense since the protagonists of the ethical model he is trying to design are also the main components of communication. Consequently, their care in the use of language must be extreme. As the direct and immediate exponents of social relations, the components of the event are necessarily obliged to follow very strict and specific verbal prescriptions.

31 Cfr. XVI, XI: 146; XX, II: 166; VI, XIX: 80.
32 Cfr. XIII, IV: 119; XIV, XXXIV: 131; XVII, III: 148; II, XXII: 59; XII, XXII: 117.
33 Cfr. I, XV: 54; XIV, XXXVII: 131; XIX, III: 159; XIX, XXV: 164; X, II: 101; X, IV: 102; XV, XXII: 139; XIV, XXII: 129; XVII, XXIV: 153; XI, IV: 106; V, VII: 72; III, XIX: 63; XV, XVIII: 138; XV, XIX: 138; XV, XXIV: 139; I, XIV: 53; I, XIII: 53; XIV, XXIII: 129; XV, VII: 136; I, II: 51; I, II: 51; XVII, XXV: 154; X, XIV: 104; IX, XXII: 99; VII, XXIV: 87; XIX, XXIV: 163; XII, II: 112; XX, I: 165; VIII, V: 91.

People who are able to avoid flattery despise worldly fame, which enables them to be polite and to concentrate on the depth of things. Moreover, because they have scrupulous respect for the past, they are accustomed to honouring their ancestors whenever they can mention them.

Beyond these specific traits, participants in communicative events focus on three major activities: they always observe the established format for each interaction, they are prudent and restrained in their use of language and they try to match their words to their acts.

In any case, the intense formalism according to Confucius' understanding of society establishes a very significant number of ritualised uses of language, especially in formal contexts, to which high dignitaries, Noblemen and even rulers are especially obliged. Participants in the communicative act have to follow specific forms. These are prefigured as binding norms of appropriate conduct in society. It is necessary to speak with reverential respect in court, which does not prevent the citizen from always expressing himself with absolute clarity and in accordance with his sincerest convictions. In the same way, there are formal rules for addressing each of the members of these estates, which are obligatory, which ends up bringing this language closer to ritual or quasi-ritual models.

Apart from the non-negotiable compliance with the established forms, Confucian civility imposes on the participants to conduct themselves linguistically with moderation, always maintaining their non-negotiable congruence with their actions. Therefore, it is a matter of nurturing a balance, which in Confucius' spiritual horizon is consubstantial to the Noble Man, capable of uniting his actions with his words.

To conclude this section, two constants in the Confucian characterisation of the participants in the communicative event should be highlighted. On the one hand, in keeping with the statal society it advocates, communication must maintain strict observance of the vertical axis of power. With such strictly marked social boundaries, verbal performance not only observes them but to a large extent also transcribes and perpetuates them. On the other hand, the participants in communicative events—as in their ethics and even in their conception of the world—are eminently male. As already mentioned, there are few references to how to address women. In any case, it does not even raise the question of what women's verbal behaviour should be.

5.3 Ends

In the *Analects* the aims revolve around two major indexes of nuclear questions both in the Confucian doctrine as a whole and in its conception of the verbal behaviour that individuals must observe. The ends are the axis that organises the whole Confucian communicative spectrum, insofar as they guide this verbal activity towards the development and consolidation of its ethical proposal.

On the one hand, the Noble Man's communication has to be congruent with his actions, one of the axes of constant presence in his approaches to linguistic behaviour (II, XIII: 57; IV, XXII: 69; XI, XXI: 110). In appearance, this is a requirement with respect to society. The Noble Man must not show several profiles, but must be consistent, unique in the message conveyed by his words and deeds. But, at the same time, it is also a personal imposition, an act of strict coherence with oneself. Hence, the well-known recommendations to match words and deeds, to listen carefully to draw consequences, and even to opt for silence when one perceives that one does not live up to these recommendations. This end directed towards the individual is a way of persevering on the Path which is proposed by its ethics.

On the other hand, linguistic behaviour must conform to the essence of names (XIII, III: 118). This is probably the most intense and imperative communicative purpose that governs Confucius' communicative doctrine. There is a certain paradox here, albeit only in appearance. It is true that he is not particularly interested in the tempestuous recesses of speculative discussion about the rightness of names. That remains for philosophy or even rhetoric, to which Confucius is so disaffected. However, there is another possible dimension related to the rightness of names (to the strict accommodation to what they should mean and the consequences derived) in the work of relations between the members of the same community. From this perspective, adjusting names to their correct semantic content is equivalent to offering reliable parameters that guarantee coexistence. Consequently, they become essential elements of civility. Hence, one of the non-negotiable aims of communication is to maintain this natural, necessary and strict equivalence.

5.4 Sequence of Acts

Apparently, this is not even a significant concern in the *Analects*. Confucius merely gives a very general recommendation about the convenience of speaking

The Contemporary Potential of the Analects: A Complex | 75

verbally in an orderly and methodical way (IX, X: 97). It is true that in many of the linguistic and communicative remarks in the *Analects* there is an implicit communicative sequence. It is true, not only in the formats of the rites that are continually appealed to but also in the interaction of the court before the sovereign, in the administration of justice or during the teachings of a master to his disciples. Perhaps, because of the contextual evidence of the sequences that per se already contain the communicative events in which Confucius thinks, he does not stop to discuss them in detail either, even if they are implicit in one way or another.

In any case, this is not the only time he does so. The *Analects* are conceived from a completely praiseworthy pedagogical practicality. Not even what is manifestly obvious is dealt with, in absolute congruence with the principle of distancing oneself from the rhetoric that the whole work advocates. To do so, to dwell on what is already known and assumed, would be a form of vain eloquence, an unnecessary waste of verbal effort that it would be worthwhile concentrating on less travelled issues.

5.5 Keys

Ethnographers of speech give an almost connotative role to linguistic cues, understood as verbal elements that mark the universe in which a linguistic action is situated. They can be used to mark the irony or severity of an intervention, the formality of a conversation, and the relations between those exchanging linguistic messages. Moreover, they do not necessarily have to be linguistic. Non-verbal elements can also qualify strictly linguistic content and, consequently, provide the necessary clues to interpret it correctly. To take a contemporary and well-known example, a lecturer may be explaining that a project was not completed due to lack of time, while at the same time using his hands to reproduce the gesture of money. The audience obviously interprets that the project ran out of budget.

The keys form an admittedly heterogeneous domain among Confucius' ethical concerns. Sometimes they are countenances, movements or attitudes that depart from violence, from displeasure. When, despite everything, these are revealed, they are immediately corrected by words. That coincides with the Confucian ideal, always polite and careful (VIII, XIV: 91). Sometimes the keys are indications to avoid rudeness, to underline the simplicity of things and of the actions of individuals, to exercise modesty or to indicate that one is on the right path of the Way.

In any case, they are not the decisive element of the communicative event as conceived by the *Analects*. Because of their own inclination towards sincerity, conceived moreover in radical terms and without possible interferences or negotiations, the keys do not cease to be an adjuvant element, valuable in that sense, although neither defining nor essential. The substance lies in the participants, in the ways in which they construct their messages and in the vital and social patterns they are capable of transmitting to others and, to no small extent, of respecting each of them when they act as speakers.

5.6 Instruments[34]

Hymes' terminology may blur the real content of this component of the event. By instruments, we mean the resources used to construct a communicative event (i.e., the different elements of the linguistic system to which the participants in the event have resorted). Of course, the type of language used is more central to the communicative concerns of the *Analects* than any of the other components.

All the precepts, prescriptions and prohibitions in the preceding sections are choices of this kind, and thus underpin Confucius' position on the appropriate forms of the message. When he recommends parsimony in the use of verbal elements, the choice of polite forms, the use of weighted words, sincerity in what is said, or that terms be adjusted to what they mean, he is proposing the selection of some linguistic resources and not others. Thus, the bulk of the communicative concern of the work is clearly concentrated in this section of the event, in accordance with the terms in which it had been formulated by Hymes.

Here, Confucius shows an extraordinary congruence once again. The forms of the message are the vectorial core to which the verbal component of ethics is

---

34 Cfr. XVII, XVIII: 152; V, XIII: 73; XVII, VIII: 157; IV, XXIV: 70; XX, III: 166; III, XV: 62; XVI, VII: 145; IV, XXVI: 70; II, II: 55; I, X: 53; XVI, XIII: 146; VII, XXX: 88; XVI, VIII: 145; VIII, IV: 91; V, IX: 73; XVI, X: 146; VI, XXIV: 81; XIX, XIII:161; V, XIV: 73; XV, XLIII: 142, XIX, IX: 160; I, III: 51; V, IV: 71; V, XXIV: 75; VI, XIV: 79; I, VII: 52; VII, XVIII: 86; XI, II: 106; X, I: 101; XV, XXVI: 139; XVI, IV: 144; XIV, V: 126; XV, X: 137; XI, XXIV: 110; XV, V: 136; XII, VIII: 114; XVII, VI: 149; XII, III: 112; XIII, XIX: 122; XI, XXV: 111; XIII, III: 118; XIII, VIII: 120; XVII, XIV: 151; XI, XXIII: 110; XIV, XXX: 130; XII, XIII: 115; XV, I: 135; XI, XIII: 108; XVI, I: 143; XVI, V: 145; XII, VI: 113; XIV, XXXIII: 131; XVII, IX: 150; XII, I: 112; XI, XX: 109.

directed. No other component of the communicative event so decisively affects an ethical mood. Of course, everything must ultimately refer to the final resultant system and the form of the messages have a certain influence. They are coordinated and complemented with the previous social relations that the participants maintain, with the use of specific keys for certain situations and scenes, with previously established sequences of acts and, in general, with the rest of the event that always develops through the coordinated interaction of its components. This does not prevent the forms of the message from being on this occasion the vector of convergence of all of them. In the end, ethical precepts lead to selecting certain components of the verbal repertoire to assembling certain discourses and behaving as speakers of one type, precisely because they are social subjects of a certain class and with certain convictions.

5.7 Standards[35]

The standards are another of the relevant sections of the *Analects* in relation to communication, more than for the volume of their contribution as a set of precepts, because they introduce nuances that are really very relevant.

In fact, everything revolves around one great rule, which is otherwise basic and immediate. The Noble Man must abide by the principles of his ethics in every aspect of his behaviour, including language. Based on this great principle, which is unquestionable, the *Analects* do introduce specific nuances, which serve as reminders of these principles applied to some specific contexts. Sometimes these are clarifications in situations where there may be hesitation to develop these precepts in concrete terms.

Thus, the *Analects* contain two broad classes of communicative rules. A relatively small group introduces very explicit and firm prescriptions. Some of these precepts govern everyday areas of life, never entirely exempt from the tenacious rigour demanded of the Noble Man. Not mentioned, neither when eating nor when in bed (IX, VIII: 103). But most of them are associated with the formal contexts of court or administration. They establish the etiquette of the names of the highest dignitaries, the drafting of official texts, how official mourning is to

---

35 XIV, IV: 125; XV, XIV: 137; XVI, XIII: 146; XVI, XIV: 147; XIV, XIV: 127; XV, XVIII: 138; XIV, IX: 126; XVI, VI: 145; XIV, XLIII: 133; XVI, XIII: 146; II, XVIII: 58; X, VIII: 103; III, XXII: 63.

be expressed, or the discretion with which officials are to behave in administrative settings.

However, such firm and clearly established guidelines are always subordinate to the exercise of good governance. If this is done in these terms, a certain condescension in the use of words is possible. Otherwise, it is imperative to adhere to socially established guidelines which, in essence, act as a guarantor that provides security for the verbal actions of individuals.

Alongside this group of formal standards, there are others of a relatively implicit type which are more oriented towards verbal behaviour in general in social life. Thus, everyday language should be free of complaints and backbiting, expressed without flattery and with respect, both towards people of knowledge and towards the past. It is advisable to speak just enough so as not to overwhelm the interlocutors, for whom the words will end up being unbearable. Of course, it is advisable to periodically introduce lofty themes, even in ordinary communication. Confucius is very persuaded of the need to do so in order not to stray from the spiritual zones that develop the figure of the Noble Man. That is why he reminds us with relative insistence of the need to be properly educated, turning to his well-known source of authority in knowledge, the everlasting Odes.

5.8 Genres

Communicative genres are not an intense concern of the *Analects* either, although they are very symptomatic of his nodal intentions. In fact, he only refers to two of them, and in a somewhat episodic manner. On the one hand, he deals with the official texts that emanate from the monarch in his governmental action, specifying the rules of protocolary elaboration, without specifying specific stylistic indications. On the other hand, he makes explicit the appropriate verbal routine in order to follow the path of wisdom that he advocates through his ethics. Only by questioning the causes of things can the individual aspire to become a Noble Man (XV, XV: 138). Of course, this is a notionally delimited genre in a very broad sense—perhaps even too broad—given that it is clearly a matter of introspection, a kind of dialogue that the individual needs to maintain with himself to pursue his itinerary of inner perfection.

This conceptual laxity, which would probably surprise some strict theorist, nevertheless underlines a very relevant fact, not only of Confucius' communicative conception, but even of the *Analects* as a whole. There are two poles around which this cautious and modest impact on communicative genres revolves: the state and the individual, alpha and omega of his ethics. The foundation of his ethics is the exemplary and elevated citizen, the final horizon that vertebrates the pyramidal society in which he believes, no less exemplary than the individual.

5.9 Event

It has already been mentioned that, ultimately, all this is articulated in a joint action of individuals in the use of human language. The last requirement of Hymes' scheme, preserving the totality of the communicative event, is thus fulfilled.

In this case, I would say that I could speak of an extended totality, as extensive as that which regulates ethical behaviour. In fact, Confucius always puts it in those terms. All the topics and aspects he deals with in his *Analects* are part of an ethical project that embraces and encompasses them all. Linguistic communication was not to be an exception. On the contrary, what we would call today a Confucian communicative event is one of his most effective and privileged instruments.

References

Hymes, D. (1974). *Foundations in sociolinguistics: An ethnographic approach.* New York: Routledge.

6

Communication as an Ethical Instrument

Any approach to Confucius ends up encountering his ethics, the very core of his thought. He conveys an obvious universalist perspective, with the inevitable nuances that the passage of time brings. Sometimes universality is seen as an ability to free oneself from the coordinates of space and time within which a work has emerged. Personally, I'm rather excepting in this respect. I understand universality in just the opposite sense. There are authors and works that continue to transmit sensations and ideas, even millennia later, as is the case with Confucius, beyond the coordinates between which they arose. But these coordinates are inevitable; they are always present, precisely because the authors and their works are a product of them. I do not understand that this involves any form of contradiction. On the contrary, I think it denotes a principle of coherence in accordance with any intellectual production and its possible projection in space and time.

Confucius and the *Analects* have been no exception. Of course, the context in which it unfolded could not be avoided. 2500 years ago, there were simply no precursors to feminism or to a society without hierarchies and classes. The sources of knowledge were canonical, and the proper performance of people was to imitate exemplary figures. But, as Khun (1962) explained, it is necessary to judge the contributions of the past from the mentality in which they were formulated. Confucius was trying to find a guideline to restore the lost order in a troubled China.

This effort is not limited to simply recovering the past. It is taken as a reference and revered with respect. But Confucius brings much more. It is not mere nostalgia that he proposes, but a path to the improvement of society, which in turn requires the improvement of every citizen.

At this point, there is a very precise and intense ethic which covers all aspects of life, from the most intimate (family life) to the great questions of state.

Communication plays a central role in this proposal, with a very comprehensive activity, again, in practically all possible areas of interaction. The Noble Man embodies the ideal virtues to which Confucius aspires. His use of language reflects, and at the same time constructs, the degree of perfection he has been able to achieve. That is why his words must reflect balance, weight, wisdom, respect and, in a broad sense, his contribution to the construction of a just state.

This commitment knows no exceptions. It binds the whole of society, starting with the humblest of disciples and ending with the sovereign himself. In the same way, access to this ethical path is also unrestricted. Anyone, from any social class, can follow it, as long as they are willing to abide by its principles.

Ultimately, what distinguishes people, what truly stratifies them, is their ability to improve themselves by adopting constructive ethics. Hence, the Noble Man is also a Superior Man, in the sense that he has been able to step out of the everyday to achieve a higher degree of self-improvement.

Precisely, the use of a particularly careful language is one of the signs of identity that distinguishes this Noble Man in society as a whole. On this point, Confucius shows an extraordinary sensitivity towards the function of language as a social stereotype, one of the most studied topics in contemporary sociolinguistics.

Of course, he will not be an isolated case. Confucius also has a clear perception about the societal nature of language, about the importance of reference persons as idiomatic models or about the cohesive value of ritual forms.

The combined result is an extraordinarily modern view of how languages work. In fact, his proposal can be framed within the parameters of the communicative event, as delimited by D. Hymes. That is why, despite the distance in time and space, Confucius continues to tell us things that are suggestive, profound and universal.

References

Kuhn, T. S. (1962). *The structure of scientific revolutions*. Chicago, IL: University of Chicago Press.

Terminology Notes

The translation options for the main terminological references in the *Analects* are given below. As can be seen, references to Spanish, English, traditional Chinese and Pinyin have been included.

Español	Inglés	Chino	Pinyín
Augusto Terrenal	**Earhtly Sovereign**	地皇	**Dìhuáng**
Analectas	**Analects**	論語	**Lún Yǔ**
Anales de Primavera y Otoño	**Spring and Autumn Annals**	春秋	**Chūnqiū**
Anyang	**Anyang**	安阳市	**Ānyáng**
Augusto Celestial	**Heavenly Sovereign**	天皇	**Tiānhuáng**
Augusto Tài	**Tai Sovereign**	泰皇	**Tàihuáng**
Chen Kang	**Chen Kang**	陳康	**Chén Kāng**
Cinco clásicos	**Five Classics**	五經	**Wǔjīng**

Español	Inglés	Chino	Pinyín
Cinco emperadores	Five Emperors	五帝	Wǔ dì
Confucio	Confucius	孔夫子	Kǒng Fūzǐ
Di ku	Ku	帝嚳	Dìkù
Han (dinastía)	Han Dynasty	漢朝	Hàncháo
Ding (duque)	Ding (duke)	齊丁公	Qí Dīng Gōng
Duanmu Ci	Duanmu Ci	端木賜	Duānmù Cì
El Justo Medio	Doctrine of the Mean	中庸	Zhōngyōng
Emperador amarillo	Yellow Emperor	黃帝	Huángdì
Erlitou (cultura)	Erlitou (culture)	二里頭文化	Èrlǐtóu wénhuà
Escuela de los Letrados	Rujia	儒家	Rújiā
Cai (estado)	Cài (state)	蔡国	Càiguó
Chen (estado)	Chen (state)	陳	Chen Guo
Chu (estado)	Chu (state)	楚	Chǔ
Song (estado)	Sòng (state)	宋	Sòng
Wei (estado)	Wei (state)	魏	Wèi
Wu (estado)	Wu (state)	吳国	Wú Guó
Feng	Feng	丰县	Fēng Xiàn
Gongshu Wenzi	Gongshu Wenzi	公叔文子	
Guo Yu	Guo Yu	國語	Guóyǔ
Han (etnia)	Han (people)	汉族	Hàn zú
Henan (provincia)	Henan (province)	河南省	Hénán Shěng

Español	Inglés	Chino	Pinyín
Huangdi	Huangdi	黄帝	Huángdì
Jiayuguan	Jiayuguan	嘉峪关市	Jiāyùguān shì
Jin (estado)	Jin (state)	晋国	Jìn Guó
Jing de Qi	Jing	齊景公	Qí Jǐng Gōng
Junzi	Junzi	君子	Jūn zǐ
Justo Medio (Teoría de la Medianía)	Doctrine of the Mean	中庸	Zhōng yōng
La Gran Enseñanza	Great Learning	大學	Dàxué
Lao-Tsé	Lao Tzu	老子	Lǎozǐ
Li	Li	禮	Lǐ
Libro de la Historia	Book of Documents	書經	Shūjīng
Libro de las odas	Classic of Poetry	詩經	Shījīng
Libro de los Ritos	Book of Rites	禮記	Lǐjì
Los Cuatro Libros	Four books	四書五經	Sìshū Wǔjīng
Lu	Lu	魯國	Lǔ Guó
Mencio (libro)	Mencius (book)	孟子	Mèngzǐ
Min Sun	Min Sun	閔損	Mǐn Sǔn
Min Sun	Min Sun	閔損	Mǐn Sǔn
Muye/Mu (batalla)	Battle of Muye (Mu)	牧野之战	Muye zhī Zhan
Pangu	Pangu	盤古	Pángǔ
Primaveras y otoños (período)	Spring and Autumn period	春秋時代	Chūn qiū shí dài;

Español	Inglés	Chino	Pinyín
Qin (dinastía)	Qin (dynasty)	秦朝	Qínchǎo
Qin Shi Huang	Qin Shi Huang	秦始皇	Qín Shǐhuáng
Qufu	Qufu	曲阜	Qūfù
Ran Qiu	Ran Qiu	冉求	Rǎn qiú
Registro del Gran Historiador	Records of the Great Historian	史記	Shǐjì
Registro del Rito	Book of Rites	禮經	Lǐjīng
Reinos combatienes (período)	Warring States period	戰國時代	Zhànguó Shídài
Río Amarillo	Yellow River	黃 河	Huáng Hé
Shandong	Shandong	山東	Shāndōng
Shang (dinastía)	Shang (dynasty)	商	Shāng
Shujing	Shujing	書經	Shūjīng
Shun	Shun	虞舜	Yúshùn
Sima Qian	Sima Qian	司馬遷,	Sīmǎ Qiān
Sima Tan	Sima Tan	司馬談	Sīmǎ Tán
Song (dinastia)	Song (dynasty)	宋朝	Sòng Cháo
Tan	Tan	譚	Tan
Ting	Ting	婷	
Tres augustos	Three Sovereigns	三皇	Sān huáng
Weri/Wey	Wey	衞	Wèi
Xia (Dinastía)	Xia (dinasty)	夏	Xià
Xiaoren	Xiaoren	小人	Xiǎorén
Xunzi	Xunzi	荀子	Xún Zǐ

Español	Inglés	Chino	Pinyín
Yan yuan	Yan yuan	颜元	Yán Yuán
Yao	Yao	唐堯	Tángyáo
Yijing	Yijing	易經	Yìjīng
Yin/yang	Yin/yang	陰|陽	Yīnyáng
Yong	Yong	勇	Yǒng
You Ruo	You Ruo	有若	Yǒu ruò
Yu el Grande	Yu the Great	大禹	Dà Yǔ
Zai Yu	Zai Yu	宰 予	Zǎi Yǔ
Zhan Xu	Zhuanxu	顓頊	Zhuānxù
Zhao (estado)	Zhao (state)	趙	Zhào
Zhao (Qi)	Zao (duke of Qi)	齊昭公	Qí Zhāo Gōng
Zheng (ducado)	Zheng	鄭	Zhèng
Zigong	Zigong	子貢	Zǐgòng
Ziyou	Ziyou	子游	Zǐyóu
Zong You	Zhong You	仲由	Zhòng Yóu
Zuo Qiuming	Zuo Qiuming	左丘明	Zuǒ Qiūmíng
Zuozhuan	Zuozhuan	左傳	Zuozhuan

PETER LANG
PROMPT

Peter Lang Prompts offer our authors the opportunity to publish original research in small volumes that are shorter and more affordable than traditional academic monographs. With a faster production time, this concise model gives scholars the chance to publish time-sensitive research, open a forum for debate, and make an impact more quickly. Like all Peter Lang publications, Prompts are thoroughly peer reviewed and can even be included in series.

For further information, please contact:

editorial@peterlang.com

To order, please contact our Customer Service Department:

peterlang@presswarehouse.com (within the U.S.)
orders@peterlang.com (outside the U.S.)

Visit our website: www.peterlang.com

Prompts include:

Claudia Aburto Guzmán, *Poesía reciente de voces en diálogo con la ascendencia hispano-hablante en los Estados Unidos: Antología breve.* ISBN 978-1-4331-5207-8. 2020

William Robert Adamson, *Mine Own Familiar Friend: The Relationship between Gerard Hopkins and Robert Bridges.* ISBN 978-1-80079-485-6. 2021

Tywan Ajani, *Barriers to Rebuilding the African American Community: Understanding the Issues Facing Today's African Americans from a Social Work Perspective.* ISBN 978-1-4331-7681-4. 2020

Macarena Areco, *Bolaño Constelaciones: Literatura, sujetos, territories.* ISBN 978-1-4331-7575-6. 2020

Robin Burgess (ed.), *FRANCESCO ALGAROTTI: AN ESSAY ON THE OPERA (Saggio sopra l'opera in musica) The editions of 1755 and 1763.* ISBN 978-1-80079-505-1. 2022

Desrine Bogle. *The Transatlantic Culture Trade: Caribbean Creole Proverbs from Africa, Europe, and the Caribbean.* ISBN 978-1-4331-5723-3. 2020

Jean-François Caron. *Irresponsible Citizenship: The Cultural Roots of the Crisis of Authority in Times of Pandemic.* ISBN 978-1-4331-8908-1. 2021

Jean-François Caron, *The Great Lockdown: Western Societies and the Fear of Death.* ISBN 978-1-4331-9535-8. 2022

Marcílio de Freitas and Marilene Corrêa da Silva Freitas, *The Future of Amazonia in Brazil: A Worldwide Tragedy.* ISBN 978-1-4331-7793-4. 2020

Mihai Dragnea. *Christian Identity Formation Across the Elbe in the Tenth and Eleventh Centuries.* Christianity and Conversion in Scandinavia and the Baltic Region, c. 800–1600, vol. 1. ISBN 978-1-4331-8431-4. 2021

Janet Farrell Leontiou, *The Doctor Still Knows Best: How Medical Culture Is Still Marked by Paternalism.* Health Communication, vol. 15. ISBN 978-1-4331-7322-6. 2020

Clare Gorman (ed.), *Miss-representation: Women, Literature, Sex and Culture.* ISBN 978-1-78874-586-4. 2020

Eva Marín Hlynsdóttir. *Gender in Organizations: The Icelandic Female Council Manager.* ISBN 978-1-4331-7729-3. 2020

Micol Kates, *Towards a Vegan-Based Ethic: Dismantling Neo-Colonial Hierarchy Through an Ethic of Lovingkindness.* ISBN 978-1-4331-7797-2. 2020

Sunho Kim, *Inner Mongolia, Outer Mongolia: The History of the Division of the "Descendants of Chinggis Khan" in the 20th Century.* ISBN 978-1-4331-8185-6. 2022

Feridoon Koohi-Kamali (ed.), *Exploring Roots of Inequality in Latin America and Peru.* ISBN 978-1-4331-8989-0. 2021

Guy Merchant, Cathy Burnett, Jeannie Bulman, and Emma Rogers. *Stacking Stories: Exploring the Hinterland of Education.* ISBN 978-1-80079-686-7. 2022

Matt Qvortrup, *Winners and Losers: Which Countries are Successful and Why?.* ISBN 978-1-80079-405-4. 2021

Peter Raina, *Doris Lessing – A Life Behind the Scenes: The Files of the British Intelligence Service MI5.* ISBN 978-1-80079-183-1. 2021

Peter Raina (trans.), *Heinrich von Kleist Poems.* ISBN 978-1-80079-043-8. 2020

Josiane Ranguin, *Mediating the Windrush Children: Caryl Phillips and Horace Ové.* ISBN 978-1-4331-7424-7. 2020

Dylan Scudder, *Coffee and Conflict in Colombia: Part of the Pentalemma Series on Managing Global Dilemmas.* ISBN 978-1-4331-7568-8. 2020

Dylan Scudder, *Conflict Minerals in the Democratic Republic of Congo: Part of the Pentalemma Series on Managing Global Dilemmas.* ISBN 978-1-4331-7561-9. 2020

Dylan Scudder, *Mining Conflict in the Philippines: Part of the Pentalemma Series on Managing Global Dilemmas.* ISBN 978-1-4331-7632-6. 2020

Dylan Scudder, *Multi-Hazard Disaster in Japan: Part of the Pentalemma Series on Managing Global Dilemmas.* ISBN 978-1-4331-7530-5. 2020

Wesley A. Stroud, *Education for Liberation, Education for Dignity: The Story of St. Monica's School of Basic Learning for Women.* ISBN 978-1-4331-7911-2. 2021

Geanneti Tavares Salomon, *Fashion and Irony in «Dom Casmurro».* ISBN 978-1-78997-972-5. 2021

Zia Ul Haque Shamsi, *South Asia Needs Hybrid Peace.* ISBN 978-1-4331-9422-1. 2022

Mohammad Rafiqul Islam Talukdar, *Local Government Budgetary Autonomy: Evidence from Bangladesh.* ISBN 978-1-80079-528-0. 2022

Shai Tubali, *Cosmos and Camus: Science Fiction Film and the Absurd.* ISBN 978-1-78997-664-9. 2020

Angela Williams, *Hip Hop Harem: Women, Rap and Representation in the Middle East.* ISBN 978-1-4331-7295-3. 2020

Ivan Zhavoronkov (trans.), *The Socio-Cultural and Philosophical Origins of Science* by Anatoly Nazirov. ISBN 978-1-4331-7228-1. 2020

www.ingramcontent.com/pod-product-compliance
Lightning Source LLC
Chambersburg PA
CBHW060318100426
42812CB00003B/818